CHILDREN'S BOOK OF CLASSIC

POEMS & RHYMES

THE COMPILER

Nicola Baxter has written and compiled over three hundred children's titles. She has developed ideas for a wide variety of international publishers and particularly enjoys the marriage of words and pictures that children's books entail.

THE ILLUSTRATOR

Cathie Shuttleworth was trained in calligraphy, heraldry and illumination. Through her work with the Royal College of Arms, she has produced coats of arms for the wedding of HRH Prince Andrew and other royal projects, but her real love is illustration, particularly of a wide range of children's books.

CHILDREN'S BOOK OF CLASSIC
POEMS & RHYMES

Illustrated by Cathie Shuttleworth

Over 135 best-loved verses from the great poets on the
themes of nature, travel, childhood, love, adventure,
sadness, happiness, magic, mystery and nonsense

ARMADILLO

This edition is published by Armadillo,
an imprint of Anness Publishing Ltd, Blaby Road,
Wigston, Leicestershire LE18 4SE; info@anness.com

www.annesspublishing.com

If you like the images in this book and would like to investigate using
them for publishing, promotions or advertising, please visit our website
www.practicalpictures.com for more information.

© Anness Publishing Ltd 2013

Publisher: Joanna Lorenz
Compiled by Nicola Baxter
Illustrated by Cathie Shuttleworth
Production Controller: Pirong Wang

PUBLISHER'S NOTE
The author and publishers have made every effort to ensure that this book is safe
for its intended use, and cannot accept any legal responsibility or liability for
any harm or injury arising from misuse.

Manufacturer: Anness Publishing Ltd,
Blaby Road, Wigston, Leicestershire LE18 4SE, England
For Product Tracking go to: www.annesspublishing.com/tracking
Batch: 6055-20931-1127

CONTENTS

ANIMALS
and
BIRDS

The Owl and the Pussy-Cat

The Owl and the Pussy-Cat went to sea
In a beautiful pea-green boat,
They took some honey, and plenty of money;
Wrapped up in a five-pound note.
The Owl looked up to the stars above,
And sang to a small guitar,
"O lovely Pussy, O Pussy, my love,
What a beautiful Pussy you are,
    You are,
    You are!
What a beautiful Pussy you are!"

Pussy said to the Owl, "You elegant fowl!
How charmingly sweet you sing!
O let us be married! too long we have tarried:
But what shall we do for a ring?"
They sailed away for a year and a day,
To the land where the Bong-tree grows,
And there in a wood a Piggy-wig stood,
With a ring at the end of his nose,
    His nose,
    His nose,
With a ring at the end of his nose.

"Dear Pig, are you willing to sell for one shilling
Your ring?" Said the Piggy, "I will."
So they took it away, and were married next day
By the Turkey who lives on the hill.
They dined on mince, and slices of quince,
Which they ate with a runcible spoon;
And hand in hand, on the edge of the sand,
They danced by the light of the moon,
  The moon,
  The moon,
They danced by the light of the moon.

Edward Lear

Jabberwocky

'Twas brillig, and the slithy toves
Did gyre and gimble in the wabe:
All mimsy were the borogoves,
And the mome raths outgrabe.

"Beware the Jabberwock, my son!
The jaws that bite, the claws that catch!
Beware the Jubjub bird, and shun
The frumious Bandersnatch!"

He took his vorpal sword in hand:
Long time the manxome foe he sought –
So rested he by the Tumtum tree,
And stood awhile in thought.

And, as in uffish thought he stood,
The Jabberwock, with eyes of flame,
Came whiffling through the tulgey wood,
And burbled as it came!

One, two! One, two! And through and through
The vorpal blade went snicker-snack!
He left it dead, and with its head
He went galumphing back.

"And hast thou slain the Jabberwock?
Come to my arms, my beamish boy!
O frabjous day! Callooh! Callay!"
He chortled in his joy.

'Twas brillig, and the slithy toves
Did gyre and gimble in the wabe:
All mimsy were the borogoves,
And the mome raths outgrabe.

Lewis Carroll

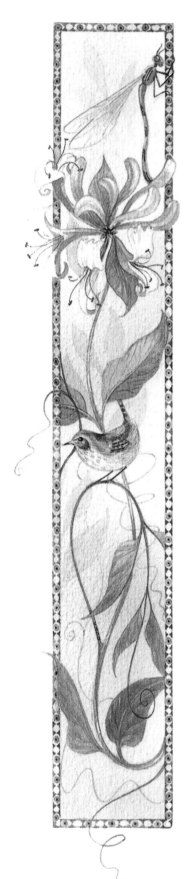

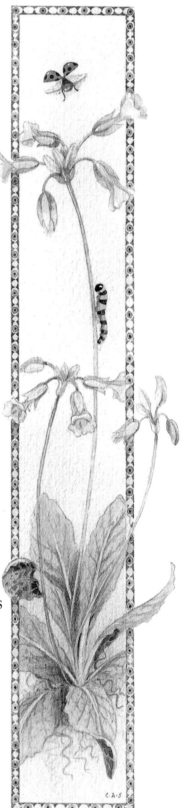

Hurt No Living Thing

Hurt no living thing;
Ladybird, nor butterfly,
Nor moth with dusty wing,
Nor cricket chirping cheerily,
Nor grasshopper so light of leap,
Nor dancing gnat, nor beetle fat,
Nor harmless worms that creep.

Christina Rossetti

Auguries of Innocence

To see a World in a Grain of Sand
And a Heaven in a Wild Flower,
Hold Infinity in the palm of your hand
And Eternity in an hour.

A Robin Red breast in a Cage
Puts all Heaven in a Rage.
A dove house fill'd with doves & Pigeons
Shudders Hell thro' all its regions.
A dog starv'd at his Master's Gate
Predicts the ruin of the State.
A Horse misus'd upon the Road
Calls to Heaven for Human blood.

Each outcry of the hunted Hare
A fibre from the Brain does tear.
A Skylark wounded in the wing,
A Cherubim does cease to sing.
The Game Cock clip'd & arm'd for fight
Does the Rising Sun affright.
Every Wolf's & Lion's howl
Raises from Hell a Human Soul.
The wild deer, wand'ring here & there,
Keeps the Human Soul from Care.
The Lamb misus'd breeds Public strife
And yet forgives the Butcher's Knife.
The Bat that flits at close of Eve
Has left the Brain that won't Believe.
The Owl that calls upon the Night
Speaks the Unbeliever's fright.
He who shall hurt the little Wren
Shall never be belov'd by Men.
He who the Ox to wrath has mov'd
Shall never be by Woman lov'd.
The wanton Boy that kills the Fly
Shall fell the Spider's enmity.
He who torments the Chafer's sprite
Weaves a Bower in endless Night.
The Catterpiller on the Leaf
Repeats to thee thy Mother's grief.
Kill not the Moth nor Butterfly,
For the Last Judgment draweth nigh.

William Blake

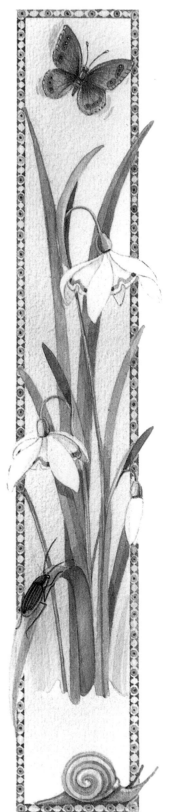

How Doth the Little Crocodile

How doth the little crocodile
Improve his shining tail;
And pour the waters of the Nile
On every golden scale!

How cheerfully he seems to grin,
How neatly spreads his claws,
And welcomes little fishes in,
With gently smiling jaws!

Lewis Carroll

The Herring Loves the Merry Moonlight

The herring loves the merry moonlight,
The mackerel loves the wind,
But the oyster loves the dredging sang,
For they come of a gentle kind.

Sir Walter Scott

The Maldive Shark

About the Shark, phlegmatical one,
Pale sot of the Maldive sea,
The sleek little pilot-fish, azure and slim,
How alert in attendance be.
From his saw-pit of mouth, from his charnel of maw
They have nothing of harm to dread,
But liquidly glide on his ghastly flank
Or before his Gorgonian head;
Or luck in the port of serrated teeth
In white triple tiers of glittering gates,
And there find a haven when peril's abroad,
An asylum in jaws of the Fates!
They are friends; and friendly they guide him to prey,
Yet never partake of the treat –
Eyes and brains to the dotard lethargic and dull,
Pale ravener of horrible meat.

Herman Melville

My Cat Jeoffry

For I will consider my cat Jeoffry.
For he is the servant of the Living God,
     duly and daily serving him.
For at the first glance of the glory of God in
     the East he worships in his way.
For is this done by wreathing his body seven
     times round with elegant quickness.
For then he leaps up to catch the musk,
     which is the blessing of God upon his prayer.
For he rolls upon prank to work it in.
For having done duty and received blessing
     he begins to consider himself.
For this he performs in ten degrees.
For first he looks upon his fore-paws to see if
     they are clean.
For secondly he kicks up behind to clear away
     there.
For thirdly he works it upon stretch with the
     fore-paws extended.
For fourthly he sharpens his paws by wood.
For fifthly he washes himself.
For sixthly he rolls upon wash.
For seventhly he fleas himself, that he may not
     be interrupted upon the beat.
For eighthly he rubs himself against a post.
For ninthly he looks up for his instructions.
For tenthly he goes in quest of food.
For having considered God and himself he will
     consider his neighbour.

For if he meets another cat he will kiss her in
  kindness.
For when he takes his prey he plays with it to
  give it chance.
For one mouse in seven escapes by his
  dallying.
For when his day's work is done his business
  more properly begins.
For he keeps the Lord's watch in the night
  against the adversary.
For he counteracts the powers of darkness
  by his electrical skin & glaring eyes.
For he counteracts the Devil, who is death,
  by brisking about the life.
For in his morning orisons he loves the sun
  and the sun loves him.
For he is of the tribe of Tiger.
For the Cherub Cat is a term of the Angel Tiger.
For he has the subtlety and hissing of a serpent,
  which in goodness he suppresses.
For he will not do destruction, if he is well-fed,
  neither will he spit without provocation.
For he purrs in thankfulness, when God tells
  him he's a good Cat.
For he is an instrument for the children to learn
  benevolence upon.
For every house is incompleat without him &
  a blessing is lacking in the spirit.

Christopher Smart

The Owl

When cats run home and light is come,
And dew is cold upon the ground,
And the far-off stream is dumb,
And the whirring sail goes round,
And the whirring sail goes round;
Alone and warming his five wits,
The white owl in the belfry sits.

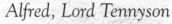

When merry milkmaids click the latch,
And rarely smells the new-mown hay,
And the cock hath sung beneath the thatch
Twice or thrice his roundelay,
Twice or thrice his roundelay;
Alone and warming his five wits,
The white owl in the belfry sits.

Alfred, Lord Tennyson

The Silver Swan

The silver swan, who living had no note,
When death approached, unlocked her silent throat,
Leaning her breast against the reedy shore,
Thus sung her first and last, and sung no more:
Farewell all joys! O death, come close mine eyes;
More geese than swans now live, more fools than wise.

Anonymous

The Eagle

He clasps the crag with crooked hands;
Close to the sun in lonely lands,
Ring'd with the azure world, he stands.

The wrinkled sea beneath him crawls;
He watches from his mountain walls,
And like a thunderbolt he falls.

Alfred, Lord Tennyson

Old Mother Goose

Old Mother Goose,
When she wanted to wander,
Would ride through the air
On a very fine gander.

Mother Goose had a house,
'Twas built in a wood,
An owl at the door
For a porter stood.

She had a son Jack,
A plain-looking lad,
He was not very good,
Nor yet very bad.

She sent him to market,
A live goose he bought:
"Here! Mother," says he,
"It will not go for naught."

Jack's goose and her gander
Grew very fond;
They'd both eat together,
Or swim in one pond.

Jack found one morning,
As I have been told,
His goose had laid him
An egg of pure gold.

Jack rode to his mother,
The news for to tell.
She called him a good boy,
And said it was well.

Anonymous

My Black Hen

Higgledy, piggledy, my black hen,
She lays eggs for gentlemen;
Gentlemen come every day
To see what my black hen doth lay.
Sometimes nine and sometimes ten,
She lays eggs for gentlemen.

Goosey Gander

Goosey, goosey, gander,
Whither shall I wander?
Upstairs, downstairs,
And in my lady's chamber.

There I met an old man,
Who wouldn't say his prayers.
I took him by the left leg
And threw him down the stairs.

26

Cock-a-doodle-do!

Cock-a-doodle-doo!
My dame has lost her shoe!
My master's lost his fiddling stick
And doesn't know what to do!

Cock-a-doodle-doo!
What is my dame to do?
Till master finds his fiddling stick,
She'll dance without her shoe!

Cock-a-doodle-doo!
My dame has found her shoe.
And master's found his fiddling stick,
Sing doodle-doodle-doo!

Cock-a-doodle-doo!
My dame will dance with you.
While master fiddles his fiddling stick
For dame and doodle-doo.

The Way We Ride

This is the way the ladies ride,
Nimble, nimble, nimble, nimble.
This is the way the gentlemen ride,
A gallop, a trot, a gallop, a trot.
This is the way the farmers ride,
Jiggety-jog, jiggety-jog.
And when they come to a hedge,
They jump over!
And when they come to a slippery space,
They scramble, scramble, scramble,
Tumble-down Dick!

Yankee Doodle

Yankee Doodle went to town,
Riding on a pony;
He stuck a feather in his cap
And called it macaroni.

Dapple Grey

I had a little pony,
His name was Dapple Grey;
I lent him to a lady,
To ride a mile away.
She whipped him,
She slashed him,
She rode him through the mire;
I would not lend my pony now,
For all the lady's hire.

Hickory, Dickory, Dock

Hickory, dickory, dock,
The mouse ran up the clock.
The clock struck one,
The mouse ran down,
Hickory, dickory, dock.

Six Little Mice

Six little mice sat down to spin;
Pussy passed by, and she peeped in.
What are you doing, my little men?
Weaving coats for gentlemen.
Shall I come in
And cut off your threads?
No, no, Mistress Pussy,
You'd bite off our heads.
Oh no, I won't,
I'll help you spin.
That may be so,
But you can't come in!

WEATHER and SEASONS

Whether the Weather Be Fine

Whether the weather be fine
Or whether the weather be not,
Whether the weather be cold
Or whether the weather be hot,
We'll weather the weather
Whatever the weather,
Whether we like it or not.

Anonymous

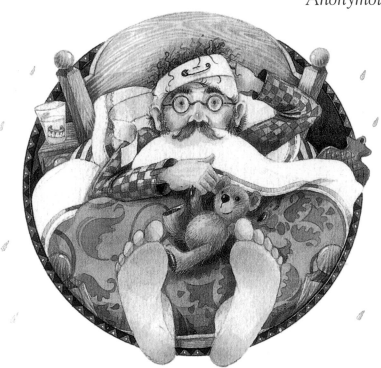

It's Raining, It's Pouring

It's raining, it's pouring,
The old man is snoring;
He went to bed and bumped his head
And couldn't get up in the morning!

Anonymous

32

The Rainbow

Boats sail on the rivers,
And ships sail on the seas;
But clouds that sail across the sky
Are prettier far than these.

There are bridges on the rivers,
As pretty as you please;
But the bow that bridges heaven,
And overtops the trees,
And builds a road from earth to sky,
Is prettier far than these.

Christina Rossetti

The Wind

Who has seen the wind?
Neither I nor you;
But when the leaves hang trembling
The wind is passing through.

Who has seen the wind?
Neither you nor I;
But when the trees bow down their heads
The wind is passing by.

Christina Rossetti

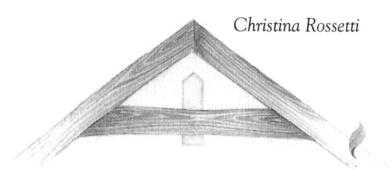

The North Wind Doth Blow

The north wind doth blow,
And we shall have snow,
And what will poor robin do then,
Poor thing?

He'll sit in a barn,
And keep himself warm,
And hide his head under his wing,
Poor thing.

Anonymous

Windy Nights

Whenever the moon and stars are set,
    Whenever the wind is high,
All night long in the dark and wet,
    A man goes riding by.
Late in the night when the fires are out,
Why does he gallop and gallop about?

Whenever the trees are crying aloud,
    And ships are tossed at sea,
By, on the highway, low and loud,
    By at the gallop goes he.
By at the gallop he goes, and then
By he comes back at the gallop again.

Robert Louis Stevenson

The Human Seasons

Four seasons fill the measure of the year;
There are four seasons in the mind of man:
He has his lusty Spring, when fancy clear
Takes in all beauty with an easy span:

He has his Summer, when luxuriously
Spring's honey'd cud of youthful thought he loves
To ruminate, and by such dreaming nigh
His nearest unto heaven: quiet coves

His soul has in its Autumn, when his wings
He furleth close; contented so to look
On mists in idleness – to let fair things
Pass by unheeded as a threshold brook:

He has his Winter too of pale misfeature,
Or else he would forgo his mortal nature.

John Keats

Winter

When icicles hang by the wall,
And Dick the shepherd blows his nail,
And Tom bears logs into the hall,
And milk comes frozen home in pail;
When blood is nipped, and ways be foul,
Then nightly sings the staring owl.
Tu-whit, tu-who! a merry note,
While greasy Joan doth keel the pot.

When all aloud the wind doth blow,
And coughing drowns the parson's saw,
And birds sit brooding in the snow,
And Marian's nose looks red and raw,
When roasted crabs hiss in the bowl,
Then nightly sings the staring owl,
Tu-whit, tu-who! a merry note,
While greasy Joan doth keel the pot.

William Shakespeare

Spring

Sound the Flute!
Now it's mute.
Birds delight
Day and Night;
Nightingale
In the dale,
Lark in Sky,
Merrily,
Merrily, Merrily, to welcome in the Year.

Little Boy,
Full of joy;
Little Girl,
Sweet and small;
Cock does crow,
So do you;
Merry voice,
Infant noise,
Merrily, Merrily, to welcome in the Year.

Little Lamb,
Here I am;
Come and lick
My white neck;
Let me pull
Your soft Wool;
Let me kiss
Your soft face:
Merrily, Merrily, we welcome in the Year.

William Blake

39

From *Rain in Summer*

How beautiful is the rain!
After the dust and heat,
In the broad and fiery street,
In the narrow lane,
How beautiful is the rain!

How it clatters along the roofs,
Like the tramp of hoofs!
How it gushes and struggles out
From the throat of the overflowing spout!

Across the window-pane
It pours and pours;
And swift and wide,
With a muddy tide,
Like a river down the gutter roars
The rain, the welcome rain!

Henry Wadsworth Longfellow

Fall, Leaves, Fall

Fall, leaves, fall: die, flowers, away;
Lengthen night and shorten day,
Every leaf speaks bliss to me
Fluttering from the autumn tree.
I shall smile when wreaths of snow
Blossom where the rose should grow;
I shall sing when night's decay
Ushers in a drearier day.

Emily Brontë

The Year's at the Spring

The year's at the spring
And day's at the morn;
Morning's at seven;
The hill-side's dew-pearled;
The lark's on the wing;
The snail's on the thorn:
God's in his heaven –
All's right with the world!

Robert Browning

BRIGHT
and
BEAUTIFUL

Pied Beauty

Glory be to God for dappled things –
For skies of couple-colour as a brinded cow;
For rose-moles all in stipple upon trout that swim;
Fresh-firecoal chestnut-falls; finches' wings;
Landscape plotted and pieced – fold, fallow, and plough;
And all trades, their gear and tackle and trim.

All things counter, original, spare, strange;
Whatever is fickle, freckled (who knows how?)
With swift, slow; sweet, sour; adazzle, dim;
He fathers-forth whose beauty is past change:
                                        Praise him

Gerard Manley Hopkins

44

Daffodils

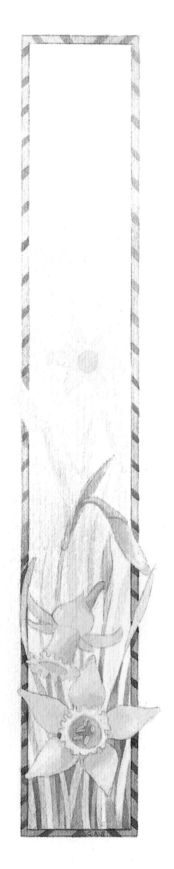

I wandered lonely as a cloud
        That floats on high o'er vales and hills,
When all at once I saw a crowd,
        A host, of golden daffodils;
Beside the lake, beneath the trees,
Fluttering and dancing in the breeze.

Continuous as the stars that shine
        And twinkle on the Milky Way,
They stretched in never-ending line
        Along the margin of a bay:
Ten thousand saw I at a glance,
Tossing their heads in sprightly dance.

The waves beside them danced, but they
        Out-did the sparkling waves in glee:
A poet could not but be gay,
        In such a jocund company:
I gazed – and gazed – but little thought
What wealth the show to me had brought:

For oft, when on my couch I lie
        In vacant or in pensive mood,
They flash upon that inward eye
        Which is the bliss of solitude;
And then my heart with pleasure fills,
And dances with the daffodils.

William Wordsworth

My Shadow

I have a little shadow that goes in and out with me,
And what can be the use of him is more than I can see.
He is very, very like me from the heels up to the head;
And I see him jump before me, when I jump into my bed.

The funniest thing about him is the way he likes to grow –
Not at all like proper children, which is always very slow;
For he sometimes shoots up taller like an india-rubber ball,
And he sometimes gets so little that there's none of him at all.

He hasn't got a notion of how children ought to play,
And can only make a fool of me in every sort of way.
He stays so close behind me he's a coward you can see;
I'd think shame to stick to nursie as that shadow sticks to me!

One morning, very early, before the sun was up,
I rose and found the shining dew on every buttercup;
But my lazy little shadow, like an arrant sleepy-head,
Had stayed at home behind me and was fast asleep in bed.

Robert Louis Stevenson

The Ecchoing Green

The sun does arise;
And make happy the skies.
The merry bells ring
To welcome the Spring;
The skylark and thrush,
The birds of the bush,
Sing louder around
To the bells' chearful sound,
While our sports shall be seen
On the Ecchoing Green.

Old John, with white hair,
Does laugh away care,
Sitting under the oak,
Among the old folk.
They laugh at our play,
And soon they all say:
"Such, such were the joys
When we all, girls & boys,
In our youth time were seen
On the Ecchoing Green."

Till the little ones, weary,
No more can be merry;
The sun does descend,
And our sports have an end.
Round the laps of their mothers
Many sisters and brothers,
Like birds in their nest,
Are ready for rest,
And sport no more seen
On the darkening Green.

William Blake

She Walks in Beauty

She walks in beauty, like the night
    Of cloudless climes and starry skies;
And all that's best of dark and bright
    Meet in her aspect and her eyes:
Thus mellowed to that tender light
    Which heaven to gaudy day denies.

One shade the more, one ray the less,
    Had half impaired the nameless grace
Which waves in every raven tress,
    Or softly lightens o'er her face;
Where thoughts serenely sweet express
    How pure, how dear their dwelling-place.

And on that cheek, and o'er that brow,
    So soft, so calm, yet eloquent,
The smiles that win, the tints that glow,
    But tell of days in goodness spent,
A mind at peace with all below,
    A heart whose love is innocent.

George Gordon, Lord Byron

Shall I Compare Thee to a Summer's Day?

Shall I compare thee to a summer's day?
 Thou art more lovely and more temperate:
Rough winds do shake the darling buds of May,
 And summer's lease hath all too short a date:
Sometime too hot the eye of heaven shines,
 And often is his gold complexion dimmed;
And every fair from fair sometime declines,
 By chance, or nature's changing course untrimmed;
But thy eternal summer shall not fade,
 Nor lose possession of that fair thou owest,
Nor shall Death brag thou wanderest in his shade,
 When in eternal lines to time thou growest;
So long as men can breathe, or eyes can see,
So long lives this, and this gives life to thee.

William Shakespeare

Blow, Bugle, Blow

The splendour falls on castle walls
    And snowy summits old in story:
The long light shakes across the lakes,
    And the wild cataract leaps in glory.
Blow, bugle, blow, set the wild echoes flying,
Blow, bugle; answer, echoes, dying, dying, dying.

O hark, O hear! how thin and clear,
    And thinner, clearer, farther going!
O sweet and far from cliff and scar
    The horns of Elfland faintly blowing!
Blow, let us hear the purple glens replying:
Blow, bugle; answer, echoes, dying, dying, dying.

O love, they die in yon rich sky,
    They faint on hill or field or river:
Our echoes roll from soul to soul,
    And grow for ever and for ever.
Blow, bugle, blow, set the wild echoes flying,
And answer, echoes, answer, dying, dying, dying.

Alfred, Lord Tennyson

DREAMS
and
WONDERS

Kubla Khan

In Xanadu did Kubla Khan
   A stately pleasure-dome decree:
Where Alph, the sacred river, ran
Through caverns measureless to man
   Down to a sunless sea.
So twice five miles of fertile ground
  With walls and towers were girdled round:
And there were gardens bright with sinuous rills
Where blossomed many an incense-bearing tree;
And here were forests ancient as the hills,
Enfolding sunny spots of greenery.

But O, that deep romantic chasm which slanted
Down the green hill athwart a cedarn cover!
A savage place! as holy and enchanted
As e'er beneath a waning moon was haunted
By woman wailing for her demon-lover!
And from this chasm, with ceaseless turmoil seething,
As if this earth in fast thick pants were breathing,
A mighty fountain momently was forced;
Amid whose swift half-intermitted burst
Huge fragments vaulted like rebounding hail,
Or chaffy grain beneath the thresher's flail:
And 'mid these dancing rocks at once and ever
It flung up momently the sacred river.
Five miles meandering with a mazy motion
Through wood and dale the sacred river ran,
Then reached the caverns measureless to man,
And sank in tumult to a lifeless ocean:
And 'mid this tumult Kubla heard from far
Ancestral voices prophesying war!

The shadow of the dome of pleasure
    Floated midway on the waves;
Where was heard the mingled measure
    From the fountain and the caves.
It was a miracle of rare device,
A sunny pleasure-dome with caves of ice!

A damsel with a dulcimer
    In a vision once I saw:
It was an Abyssinian maid,
    And on her dulcimer she played,
Singing of Mount Abora.
Could I revive within me,
    Her symphony and song,
To such a deep delight 'twould win me,
That with music loud and long,
I would build that dome in air,
That sunny dome! those caves of ice!
And all who heard should see them there,
And all should cry, Beware! Beware!
His flashing eyes, his floating hair!
    Weave a circle round him thrice,
        And close your eyes with holy dread,
For he on honey-dew hath fed,
    And drunk the milk of Paradise.

Samuel Taylor Coleridge

La Belle Dame Sans Merci

O what can ail thee, knight-at-arms,
Alone and palely loitering?
The sedge has wither'd from the lake,
And no birds sing.

O what can ail thee, knight-at-arms,
So haggard and so woe-begone?
The squirrel's granary is full,
And the harvest's done.

I see a lily on thy brow,
With anguish moist and fever dew;
And on thy cheeks a fading rose
Fast withereth too.

I met a lady in the meads,
Full beautiful – a faery's child,
Her hair was long, her foot was light,
And her eyes were wild.

I made a garland for her head,
And bracelets too, and fragrant zone;
She look'd at me as she did love,
And made sweet moan.

I set her on my pacing steed,
And nothing else saw all day long;
For sidelong would she bend, and sing
A faery's song.

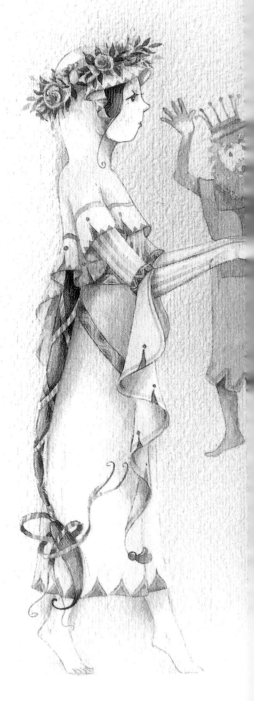

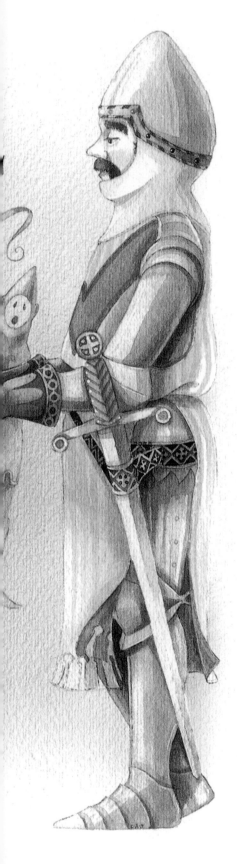

She found me roots of relish sweet,
And honey wild, and manna dew,
And sure in language strange she said –
"I love thee true".

She took me to her elfin grot,
And there she wept and sigh'd full sore,
And there I shut her wild wild eyes
With kisses four.

And there she lulled me asleep
And there I dream'd – Ah! woe betide!
The latest dream I ever dream'd
On the cold hill side.

I saw pale kings and princes too,
Pale warriors, death-pale were they all;
They cried – "La Belle Dame sans Merci
Hath thee in thrall!"

I saw their starved lips in the gloam,
With horrid warning gaped wide,
And I awoke and found me here,
On the cold hill's side.

And this is why I sojourn here
Alone and palely loitering,
Though the sedge has wither'd from the lake,
And no birds sing.

John Keats

I Saw a Peacock

I saw a peacock with a fiery tail
I saw a blazing comet drop down hail
I saw a cloud wrapped with ivy round
I saw an oak creep upon the ground
I saw a pismire swallow up a whale
I saw the sea brimful of ale
I saw a Venice glass full fifteen feet deep
I saw a well full of men's tears that weep
I saw red eyes all of a flaming fire
I saw a house bigger than the moon and higher
I saw the sun at twelve o'clock at night
I saw the man that saw this wondrous sight.

Anonymous

A Child's Thought

At seven, when I go to bed,
I find such pictures in my head:
Castles with dragons prowling round,
Gardens where magic fruits are found;
Fair ladies prisoned in a tower,
Or lost in an enchanted bower;
While gallant horsemen ride by streams
That border all this land of dreams
I find, so clearly in my head
At seven, when I go to bed.

Robert Louis Stevenson

SONGS
of
THE SEA

Full Fathom Five

Full fathom five they father lies;
    Of his bones are coral made;
Those are pearls that were his eyes:
    Nothing of him that doth fade,
But doth suffer a sea-change
Into something rich and strange:
Sea nymphs hourly ring his knell.
              Ding-dong!
Hark! now I hear them,
          Ding-dong, bell!

William Shakespeare

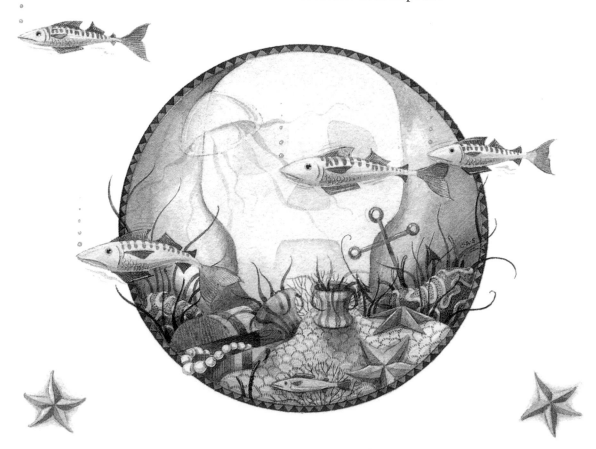

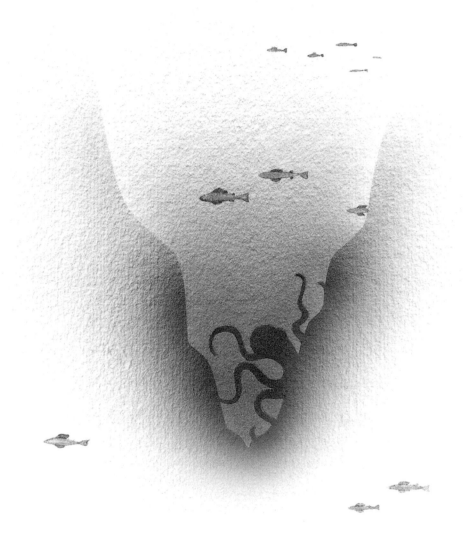

What Are Heavy?

What are heavy? sea-sand and sorrow:
What are brief? today and tomorrow:
What are frail? Spring blossoms and youth:
What are deep? the ocean and truth.

Christina Rossetti

Break, Break, Break

Break, break, break,
    On thy cold gray stones, O Sea!
And I would that my tongue could utter
    The thoughts that arise in me.

O well for the fisherman's boy,
    That he shouts with his sister at play!
O well for the sailor lad,
    That he sings in his boat on the bay!

And the stately ships go on
    To their haven under the hill;
But O for the touch of a vanish'd hand,
    And the sound of a voice that is still!

Break, break, break,
    At the foot of thy crags, O sea!
But the tender grace of a day that is dead
    Will never come back to me.

Alfred, Lord Tennyson

Monday's Child

Monday's child is fair of face,
Tuesday's child is full of grace,
Wednesday's child is full of woe,
Thursday's child has far to go,
Friday's child is loving and giving,
Saturday's child works hard for his living,
And the child that is born on the Sabbath day
Is bonny and blithe, and good and gay.

Anonymous

A Child's Grace

Here a little child I stand
Heaving up my either hand;
Cold as paddocks though they be,
Here I lift them up to Thee,
For a benison to fall
On our meat and on us all.
            Amen.

Robert Herrick

I Remember, I Remember

I remember, I remember,
The house where I was born,
The little window where the sun
Came peeping in at morn;
He never came a wink too soon,
Nor brought too long a day,
But now, I often wish the night
Had borne my breath away!

I remember, I remember,
The roses, red and white,
The violets, and the lily-cups,
Those flowers made of light!
The lilacs where the robin built,
And where my brother set
The laburnum on his birthday –
The tree is living yet!

I remember, I remember,
Where I was used to swing,
And thought the air must rush as fresh
To swallows on the wing;
My spirit flew in feathers then,
That is so heavy now,
And summer pools could hardly cool
The fever on my brow!

I remember, I remember,
The fir trees dark and high;
I used to think their slender tops
Were close against the sky:
It was a childish ignorance,
But now 'tis little joy
To know I'm farther off from Heav'n
Than when I was a boy.

Thomas Hood

Swing, Swing,

Swing, swing,
Sing, sing,
Here! my throne and I am a king!
Swing, swing,
Sing, sing,
Farewell, earth, for I'm on the wing!

Low, high,
Here I fly,
Like a bird through sunny sky;
Free, free,
Over the lea,
Over the mountain, over the sea!

Soon, soon,
Afternoon,
Over the sunset, over the moon;
Far, far,
Over all bar,
Sweeping on from star to star!

No, no,
Low, low,
Sweeping daisies with my toe.
Slow, slow,
To and fro,
Slow – slow – slow – slow.

William Allingham

Escape at Bedtime

The lights from the parlour and kitchen shone out
    Through the blinds and the windows and bars;
And high overhead and all moving about,
    There were thousands of millions of stars.
There ne'er were such thousands of leaves on a tree,
    Nor of people in church or the Park,
As the crowds of the stars looked down upon me,
    And that glittered and winked in the dark.

The Dog, and the Plough, and the Hunter, and all,
    And the star of the sailor, and Mars,
These shone in the sky, and the pail by the wall
    Would be half full of water and stars.
They saw me at last, and they chased me with cries,
    And they soon had me packed into bed;
But the glory kept shining and bright in my eyes,
    And the stars going round in my head.

Robert Louis Stevenson

Bed in Summer

In winter I get up at night
And dress by yellow candle-light.
In summer, quite the other way,
I have to go to bed by day.

I have to go to bed and see
The birds still hopping on the tree,
Or hear the grown-up people's feet
Still going past me in the street.

And does it not seem hard to you,
When all the sky is clear and blue,
And I should like so much to play,
To have to go to bed by day?

Robert Louis Stevenson

Is the Moon Tired?

Is the moon tired? She looks so pale
    Within her misty veil;
She scales the sky from east to west,
    And takes no rest.

Before the coming of the night
    The moon shows papery white;
Before the dawning of the day
    She fades away.

Christina Rossetti

Wynken, Blynken, and Nod

Wynken, Blynken, and Nod one night
Sailed off in a wooden shoe –
Sailed on a river of crystal light,
Into a sea of dew.
"Where are you going, and what do you wish?"
The old moon asked the three.
"We have come to fish for the herring fish
That live in this beautiful sea;
Nets of silver and gold have we!"
    Said Wynken,
    Blynken,
    And Nod.

The old moon laughed and sang a song
As they rocked in the wooden shoe,
And the wind that sped them all night long
Ruffled the waves of dew.
The little stars were the herring fish
That lived in that beautiful sea –
"Now cast your nets wherever you wish –
Never afeard are we";
So cried the stars to the fishermen three:
    Wynken,
    Blynken,
    And Nod.

All night long their nets they threw
To the stars in the twinkling foam –
Then down from the skies came the wooden shoe,
Bringing the fishermen home;
'Twas all so pretty a sail it seemed
As if it could not be,
And some folks thought 'twas a dream they'd dreamed
Of sailing that beautiful sea –
But I shall name you the fishermen three:
    Wynken,
    Blynken,
    And Nod.

Wynken and Blynken are two little eyes,
And Nod is a little head,
And the wooden shoe that sailed the skies
Is a wee one's trundle-bed.
So shut your eyes while mother sings
Of wonderful sights that be,
And you shall see the beautiful things
As you rock in the misty sea,
Where the old shoe rocked the fishermen three:
    Wynken,
    Blynken,
    And Nod.

Eugene Field

Star Light, Star Bright

Star light, star bright,
First star I see tonight,
I wish I may, I wish I might,
Have the wish I wish tonight.

Anonymous

How Many Miles to Babylon?

How many miles to Babylon?
    Three score miles and ten.
Can I get there by candlelight?
    Yes, and back again.
    If your heels are nimble and light,
    You may get there by candlelight.

Anonymous

98

Hush Little Baby

Hush little baby, don't say a word,
Papa's going to buy you a mockingbird.

If that mockingbird won't sing,
Papa's going to buy you a diamond ring.

If that diamond ring turns brass,
Papa's going to buy you a looking glass.

If that looking glass gets broke,
Papa's going to buy you a billy goat.

If that billy goat won't pull,
Papa's going to buy you a cart and bull.

If that cart and bull fall down,
You'll still be the sweetest little baby in town.

Anonymous

Sleep, Baby, Sleep!

Sleep, baby, sleep!
Your father herds his sheep:
Your mother shakes the little tree
From which fall pretty dreams on thee;
Sleep, baby, sleep!

Sleep, baby, sleep!
The heavens are white with sheep:
For they are lambs – those stars so bright:
And the moon's shepherd of the night;
Sleep, baby, sleep!

Sleep, baby, sleep!
And I'll give thee a sheep,
Which, with its golden bell, shall be
A little play-fellow for thee;
Sleep, baby, sleep!

Sleep, baby, sleep!
And bleat not like a sheep,
Or else the shepherd's angry dog
Will come and bite my naughty rogue;
Sleep, baby, sleep!

Sleep, baby, sleep!
Go out and herd the sheep,
Go out, you barking black dog, go,
And waken not my baby so;
Sleep, baby, sleep!

Anonymous

Love
and
Adventure

Robin Hood

In Sherwood lived stout Robin Hood,
　　An Archer great none greater.
His bow and shafts were sure and good,
　　Yet Cupid's were much better.
Robin could shoot at many a Hart and miss,
　　Cupid at first could hit a heart of his.
　　　　Hey jolly Robin,
　　　　Hoe jolly Robin,
　　　　Hey jolly Robin Hood,
　　　　Love finds out me
　　　　As well as thee
　　　　To follow me to the green wood.

A noble thief was Robin Hood,
    Wise was he could deceive him,
Yet Marian in his bravest mood
    Could of his heart bereave him,
No greater thief lies hidden under skies
    Than beauty closely lodged in women's eyes.
        Hey jolly Robin,
        Hoe jolly Robin,
        Hey jolly Robin Hood,
        Love finds out me
        As well as thee
        To follow me to the green wood.

Robert Jones

A Red, Red Rose

My love is like a red, red rose
    That's newly sprung in June:
My love is like the melody
    That's sweetly played in tune.

As fair art thou, my bonnie lass,
    So deep in love am I:
And I will love thee still, my dear,
    Till a' the seas gang dry.

Till a' the seas gang dry, my dear,
    And the rocks melt wi' the sun:
And I will love thee still, my dear,
    While the sands o' life shall run.

And fare thee weel, my only love,
    And fare thee weel a while!
And I will come again, my love,
    Thou' it were ten thousand mile.

Robert Burns

A Birthday

My heart is like a singing bird
    Whose nest is in a watered shoot;
My heart is like an apple-tree
    Whose boughs are bent with thickset fruit;
My heart is like a rainbow shell
    That paddles in a halcyon sea;
My heart is gladder than all these
    Because my love is come to me.

Raise me a dais of silk and down;
    Hang it with vair and purple dyes;
Carve it in doves and pomegranates,
    And peacocks with a hundred eyes;
Work it in gold and silver grapes,
    In leaves and silver fleurs-de-lys;
Because the birthday of my life
    Is come, my love is come to me.

Christina Rossetti

Lochinvar

O, young Lochinvar is come out of the west,
Through all the wide Border his steed was the best;
And save his good broadsword he weapons had none,
He rode all unarmed, and he rode all alone.
So faithful in love, and so dauntless in war,
There never was knight like the young Lochinvar.

He stayed not for brake, and he stopped not for stone,
He swam the Eske river where ford there was none;
But ere he alighted at Netherby gate,
The bride had consented, the gallant came late:
For a laggard in love, and a dastard in war,
Was to wed the fair Ellen of brave Lochinvar.

So boldly he entered the Netherby Hall,
Among bride's-men, and kinsmen, and brothers, and all:
Then spoke the bride's father, his hand on his sword,
(For the poor craven bridegroom said never a word)
"O come ye in peace here, or come ye in war,
Or to dance at our bridal, young Lord Lochinvar?"

"I long wooed your daughter, my suit you denied –
Love swells like the Solway, but ebbs like its tide –
And now am I come, with this lost love of mine,
To lead but one measure, drink one cup of wine.
There are maidens in Scotland more lovely by far,
That would gladly be bride to the young Lochinvar."

The bride kissed the goblet: the knight took it up,
He quaffed off the wine, and he threw down the cup.
She looked down to blush, and she looked up to sigh,
With a smile on her lips, and a tear in her eye.
He took her soft hand, ere her mother could bar,
"Now tread we a measure!" said the young Lochinvar.

So stately his form and so lovely her face,
That never a hall such a galliard did grace;
While her mother did fret, and her father did fume,
And the bridegroom stood dangling his bonnet and plume;
And the bride-maidens whispered, "'Twere better by far,
To have matched our fair cousin with young Lochinvar."

One touch to her hand, and one word in her ear,
When they reached the hall-door, and the charger stood near;
So light to the croup the fair lady he swung,
So light to the saddle before her he sprung!
"She is won! we are gone, over bank, bush, and scaur;
They'll have fleet steeds that follow," quoth young Lochinvar.

There was mounting 'mong Graemes of the Netherby clan;
Forsters, Fenwicks, and Musgraves, they rode and they ran:
There was racing and chasing on Cannobie Lee,
But the lost bride of Netherby n'er did they see.
So daring in love, and so dauntless in war,
Have ye e'er hard of gallant like young Lochinvar?

Sir Walter Scott

A New Courtly Sonnet of the Lady Greensleeves

Alas, my Love! ye do me wrong
To cast me off discourteously;
And I have loved you so long,
Delighting in your company.
  Greensleeves was all my joy,
  Greensleeves was my delight;
  Greensleeves was my heart of gold,
  And who but my Lady Greensleeves.

I have been ready at your hand,
To grant whatever you would crave;
I have both waged life and land,
Your love and goodwill for to have.

I bought thee kerchers to thy head,
That were wrought fine and gallantly;
I kept thee both at board and bed,
Which cost my purse well favouredly.

I bought thee petticoats of the best,
The cloth so fine as fine might be;
I gave thee jewels for thy chest,
And all this cost I spent on thee.

Thy purse and eke thy gay gild knives,
Thy pincase gallant to the eye;
No better wore the burgess wives,
And yet thou wouldst not love me.

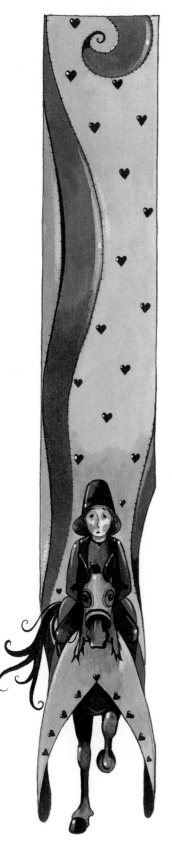

Thy gown was of the grassy green,
Thy sleeves of satin hanging by,
Which made thee be our harvest queen,
And yet thou wouldst not love me.

My gayest gelding I thee gave,
To ride wherever liked thee;
No lady ever was so brave,
And yet thou wouldst not love me.

My men were clothed all in green,
And they did ever wait on thee;
All this was gallant to be seen,
And yet thou wouldst not love me.

For every morning when thou rose,
I sent thee dainties orderly,
To cheer thy stomach from all woes,
And yet thou wouldst not love me.

Well, I will pray to God on high,
That thou my constancy mayst see,
And that yet once before I die,
Thou wilt vouchsafe to love me.

Greensleeves, now farewell! adieu!
God I pray to prosper thee;
For I am still thy lover true.
Come once again and love me.
  Greensleeves was all my joy, etc.

*Anonymous,
but some say
King Henry VIII*

The Night Has a Thousand Eyes

The night has a thousand eyes,
    And the day but one;
Yet the light of the bright world dies
    With the dying sun.

The mind has a thousand eyes,
    And the heart but one;
Yet the light of a whole life dies
    When love is done.

Francis William Bourdillon

SONGS
and
BALLADS

Thomas the Rhymer

True Thomas lay o'er yond grassy bank,
    And he beheld a ladie gay,
A ladie that was brisk and bold,
    Come riding o'er the fernie brae.

Her skirt was of the grass-green silk,
    Her mantel of the velvet fine,
At ilka tett of her horse's mane
    Hung fifty silver bells and nine.

True Thomas he took off his hat,
    And bowed him low down till his knee:
All hail, thou mighty Queen of Heaven!
    For your peer on earth I never did see.

O no, O no, True Thomas, she says,
    That name does not belong to me;
I am but the queen of fair Elfland,
    And I'm come here for to visit thee.

But ye maun go wi' me now, Thomas,
　　True Thomas, ye maun go wi' me,
For ye maun serve me seven years,
　　Thro weel or wae as may chance to be.

She turned about her milk-white steed,
　　And took True Thomas up behind,
And aye whene'er her bridle rang,
　　The steed flew swifter than the wind.

O they rade on, and further on,
　　Until they came to a garden green:
Light down, light down, ye ladie free,
　　Some of that fruit let me pull to thee.

O no, O no, True Thomas, she says,
　　That fruit maun not be touched by thee,
For a' the plagues that are in hell
　　Light on the fruit of this countrie.

But I have a loaf here in my lap,
    Likewise a bottle of claret wine,
And now ere we go farther on,
    We'll rest a while, and ye may dine.

When he had eaten and drunk his fill,
    Lay down your head upon my knee,
The lady sayd, ere we climb yon hill,
    And I will show you fairlies three.

O see not ye yon narrow road,
    So thick beset wi' thorns and briers?
That is the path of righteousness,
    Tho after it but few enquires.

And see not ye that braid braid road,
    That lies across yon lillie leven?
That is the path of wickedness,
    Tho some call it the road to heaven.

And see not ye that bonny road,
    Which winds about the fernie brae?
That is the road to fair Elfland,
    Where you and I this night maun gae.

But Thomas, ye maun hold your tongue,
    Whatever you may hear or see,
For gin ae word you should chance to speak,
    You will ne'er get back to your ain countrie.

For forty days and forty nights
    He wade thro red blude to the knee,
And he saw neither sun nor moon,
    But heard the roaring of the sea.

He has gotten a coat of the even cloth,
    And a pair of shoes of velvet green,
And till seven years were past and gone
    True Thomas on earth was never seen.

Anonymous

Bonny Barbara Allan

It was in and about the Martinmas time,
    When the green leaves were a-falling,
That Sir John Graeme in the West Country
    Fell in love with Barbara Allan.

He sent his man down through the town,
    To the place where she was dwelling,
O haste, and come to my master dear,
    Gin ye be Barbara Allan.

O hooly, hooly rose she up,
    To the place where he was lying,
And when she drew the curtain by,
    Young man, I think you're dying.

O it's I'm sick, and very very sick,
    And 'tis a' for Barbara Allan,
O the better for me ye's never be,
    Tho your heart's blood were a-spilling.

O dinna ye mind, young man, said she,
    When ye was in the tavern a-drinking,
That ye made the healths gae round and round,
    And slighted Barbara Allan?

He turned his face unto the wall,
　　And death was with him dealing;
Adieu, adieu, my dear friends all,
　　And be kind to Barbara Allan.

And slowly, slowly raise she up,
　　And slowly, slowly left him;
And sighing, said, she could not stay,
　　Since death of life had reft him.

She had not gane a mile but twa,
　　When she heard the dead-bell ringing,
And every jow that the dead-bell gied,
　　It cry'd, Woe to Barbara Allan.

O mother, mother, make my bed,
　　O make it saft and narrow,
Since my love died for me today,
　　I'll die for him tomorrow.

Anonymous

Then he gave a hitch to his trousers, which
    Is a trick all seamen larn,
And having got rid of a thumping quid,
    He spun this painful yarn:

"'Twas in the good ship *Nancy Bell*
    That we sailed to the Indian sea
And there on a reef we come to grief,
    Which has often occurred to me.

"And pretty nigh all o' the crew was drowned
    (There was seventy-seven o' soul),
And only ten of the *Nancy's* men
    Said 'Here!' to the muster-roll.

"There was me and the cook and the captain bold,
    And the mate of the *Nancy* brig,
And a bo'sun tight, and a midshipmite,
    And the crew of the captain's gig.

"For a month we'd neither wittles nor drink,
    Till a-hungry we did feel,
So we drawed a lot, and accordin' shot
    The captain for our meal.

"The next lot fell to the *Nancy's* mate,
　　And a delicate dish he made;
Then our appetite with the midshipmite
　　We seven survivors stayed.

"And then we murdered the bo'sun tight,
　　And he much resembled pig;
Then we wittled free, did the cook and me,
　　On the crew of the captain's gig.

"Then only the cook and me was left,
　　And the delicate question, 'Which
Of us two goes to the kettle?' arose,
　　And we argued it out as sich.

"For I loved that cook as a brother, I did,
　　And the cook he worshipped me;
But we'd both be blowed if we'd either be stowed
　　In the other chap's hold, you see.

"'I'll be eat if you dines off me,' says Tom,
　　'Yes, that,' says I, 'you'll be,' –
'I'm boiled if I die, my friend,' quoth I,
　　And 'Exactly so,' quoth he.

The False Knight and the Wee Boy

"O whare are ye gaun?"
    Quo' the fause knicht upon the road:
"I'm gaun to the scule,"
    Quo' the wee boy, and still he stude.

"What is that upon your back?"
    Quo' the fause knicht upon the road:
"Atweel it is my bukes,"
    Quo' the wee boy, and still he stude.

"Wha's aucht thae sheep?"
    Quo' the fause knicht upon the road:
"They are mine and my mither's,"
    Quo' the wee boy, and still he stude.

"How mony o' them are mine?"
    Quo' the fause knicht upon the road:
"A' they that hae blue tails,"
    Quo' the wee boy, and still he stude.

"I wiss ye were on yon tree,"
    Quo' the fause knicht upon the road:
"And for you to fa' down,"
    Quo' the wee boy, and still he stude.

"I wiss ye were in yon sie,"
    Quo' the fause knicht upon the road:
"And a gude bottom under me,"
    Quo' the wee boy, and still he stude.

"And the bottom for to break,"
  Quo' the fause knicht upon the road:
"*And ye to be drowned,*"
  Quo' the wee boy, and still he stude.

Anonymous

Children

Come to me, O ye children!
　　For I hear you at your play,
And the questions that perplexed me
　　Have vanished quite away.

Ye open the eastern windows,
　　That look towards the sun,
Where thoughts are singing swallows
　　And the brooks of morning run.

In your hearts are the birds and the sunshine,
　　In your thoughts the brooklet's flow,
But in mine is the wind of Autumn
　　And the first fall of the snow.

Ah! what would the world be to us
　　If the children were no more?
We should dread the desert behind us
　　Worse than the dark before.

What the leaves are to the forest,
　　With light and air for food,
Ere their sweet and tender juices
　　Have been hardened into wood –

That to the world are children;
　　Through them it feels the glow
Of a brighter and sunnier climate
　　Than reaches the trunks below.

Come to me, O ye children!
    And whisper in my ear
What the birds and the winds are singing
    In your sunny atmosphere.

For what are all our contrivings,
    And the wisdom of our books,
What compared with your caresses,
    And the gladness of your looks?

Ye are better than all the ballads
    That ever were sung or said;
For ye are living poems,
    And all the rest are dead.

Henry Wadsworth Longfellow

When That I Was and a Little Tiny Boy

When that I was and a little tiny boy,
    With hey, ho, the wind and the rain;
A foolish thing was but a toy,
    For the rain it raineth every day.

For when I came to man's estate,
    With hey, ho, the wind and the rain;
'Gainst knaves and thieves men shut their gate,
    For the rain it raineth every day.

But when I came, alas! to wive,
    With hey, ho, the wind and the rain;
By swaggering could I never thrive,
    For the rain it raineth every day.

But when I came unto my beds,
    With hey, ho, the wind and the rain;
With toss-pots still had drunken heads,
    For the rain it raineth every day.

A great while ago the world begun,
    With hey, ho, the wind and the rain;
But that's all one, our play is done,
    And we'll strive to please you every day.

William Shakespeare

MAGIC
and
MYSTERY

Waltzing Matilda

Once a jolly swagman camped by a billabong,
    Under the shade of a coolabah tree;
And he sang as he watched and waited till his billy boiled,
    "You'll come a-waltzing Matilda with me!"

"Waltzing Matilda, Waltzing Matilda,
    You'll come a-waltzing Matilda with me,"
And he sang as he watched and waited till his billy boiled,
    "You'll come a-waltzing Matilda with me."

Down came a jumbuck to drink at the billabong,
    Up jumped the swagman and grabbed him with glee;
And he sang as he shoved that jumbuck in his tucker-bag,
    "You'll come a-waltzing Matilda with me."

"Waltzing Matilda, Waltzing Matilda,
    You'll come a-waltzing Matilda with me,"
And he sang as he shoved that jumbuck in his tucker-bag,
    "You'll come a-waltzing Matilda with me."

Up rode the squatter mounted on his thoroughbred;
    Down came the troopers – one, two and three.
"Whose the jolly jumbuck you've got in your tucker-bag?
    You'll come a-waltzing Matilda with me."

"Waltzing Matilda, Waltzing Matilda,
    You'll come a-waltzing Matilda with me,
Whose the jolly jumbuck you've got in your tucker-bag?
    You'll come a-waltzing Matilda with me."

Up jumped the swagman, sprang into the billabong,
  "You'll never catch me alive," said he.
And his ghost may be heard as you pass by that billabong,
  "Who'll come a-waltzing Matilda with me?"

"Waltzing Matilda, Waltzing Matilda,
  You'll come a-waltzing Matilda with me,"
And his ghost may be heard as you pass by that billabong,
  "Who'll come a-waltzing Matilda with me?"

A. B. Paterson

The Ghost's Song

Wae's me! wae's me!
The acorn's not yet
Fallen from the tree
That's to grow the wood,
That's to make the cradle,
That's to rock the bairn,
That's to grow a man,
That's to lay me.

Anonymous

John Barleycorn

There was three Kings into the east,
    Three Kings both great and high,
And they hae sworn a solemn oath
    John Barleycorn should die.

They took a plough and plough'd him down,
    Put clods upon his head,
And they hae sworn a solemn oath
    John Barleycorn was dead.

But the cheerfu' Spring came kindly on,
    And show'rs began to fall;
John Barleycorn got up again,
    And sore surprised them all.

The sultry suns of Summer came,
    And he grew thick and strong,
His head weel arm'd wi' pointed spears,
    That no one should him wrong.

The sober Autumn enter'd mild,
    When he grew wan and pale;
His bending joints and drooping head
    Show'd he began to fail.

His colour sicken'd more and more,
    He faded into age;
And then his enemies began
    To shew their deadly rage.

They've ta'en a weapon, long and sharp,
    And cut him by the knee;
Then tied him fast upon a cart,
    Like a rogue for forgerie.

They laid him down upon his back,
    And cudgell'd him full sore;
They hung him up before the storm,
    And turn'd him o'er and o'er.

They filled up a darksome pit
    With water to the brim,
They heaved in John Barleycorn,
    There let him sink or swim.

They laid him out upon the floor,
    To work him farther woe,
And still, as signs of life appear'd,
    They toss'd him to and fro.

They wasted, o'er a scorching flame,
    The marrow of his bones;
But a miller us'd him worst of all,
    For he crush'd him between two stones.

And they hae ta'en his very heart's blood,
    And drank it round and round;
And still the more and more they drank,
    Their joy did more abound.

John Barleycorn was a hero bold,
　　Of noble enterprise,
For if you do but taste his blood,
　　'Twill make your courage rise;

'Twill make a man forget his woe;
　　'Twill heighten all his joy:
'Twill make the widow's heart to sing,
　　Tho' the tear were in her eye.

Then let us toast John Barleycorn,
　　Each man a glass in hand;
And may his great posterity
　　Ne'er fail in old Scotland!

Robert Burns

A Strange Visitor

A wife was sitting at her reel ae night;
And aye she sat, and aye she reeled, and aye she wished for company.

In came a pair o' braid braid soles, and sat down at the fireside;
And aye she sat, and aye she reeled, and aye she wished for company.

In came a pair o' sma' sma' legs, and sat down on the braid braid soles;
And aye she sat, and aye she reeled, and aye she wished for company.

In came a pair o' muckle muckle knees, and sat down on the sma' sma' legs;
And aye she sat, and aye she reeled, and aye she wished for company.

In came a pair o' sma' sma' thees, and sat down on the muckle muckle knees;
And aye she sat, and aye she reeled, and aye she wished for company.

In came a pair o' muckle muckle hips, and sat down on the sma' sma' thees;
And aye she sat, and aye she reeled, and aye she wished for company.

In came a sma' sma' waist, and sat down on the muckle muckle hips;
And aye she sat, and aye she reeled, and aye she wished for company.

In came a pair o' braid braid shouthers, and sat down on the sma' sma' waist;
And aye she sat, and aye she reeled, and aye she wished for company.

In came a pair o' sma' sma' arms, and sat down on the braid braid shouthers;
And aye she sat, and aye she reeled, and aye she wished for company.

In came a pair o' muckle muckle hands, and sat down on the sma' sma' arms;
And aye she sat, and aye she reeled, and aye she wished for company.

In came a sma' sma' neck, and sat down on the braid braid shouthers;
And aye she sat, and aye she reeled, and aye she wished for company.

In came a great big head, and sat down on the sma' sma' neck;
And aye she sat, and aye she reeled, and aye she wished for company.

"What way hae ye sic braid braid feet?" quo' the wife.
"Muckle ganging, muckle ganging."
"What way hae ye sic sma' sma' legs?"
"*Aih-h-h!* – late – and *wee-e-e* moul."
"What way hae ye sic muckle muckle knees?"
"Muckle praying, muckle praying."
"What way hae ye sic sma' sma' thees?"
"*Aih-h-h!* – late – and *wee-e-e* moul."
"What way hae ye sic big big hips?"
"Muckle sitting, muckle sitting."
"What way hae ye sic a sma' sma' waist?"
"*Aih-h-h!* – late – and *wee-e-e* moul."
"What way hae ye sic braid braid shouthers?"
"Wi' carrying broom, wi' carrying broom."
"What way hae ye sic sma' sma' arms?"
"*Aih-h-h!* – late – and *wee-e-e* moul."
"What way hae ye sic muckle muckle hands?"
"Threshing wi' an iron flail, threshing wi' an iron flail."
"What way hae ye sic a sma' sma' neck?"
"*Aih-h-h!* – late – and *wee-e-e* moul."
"What way hae ye sic a muckle muckle head?"
"Muckle wit, muckle wit."
"What do you come for?"
"For YOU!"

Anonymous

145

The Oxen

Christmas Eve, and twelve of the clock.
    "Now they are all on their knees,"
An elder said as we sat in a flock
    By the embers in hearthside ease.

We pictured the meek mild creatures where
    They dwelt in their strawy pen,
Nor did it occur to one of us there
    To doubt they were kneeling then.

So fair a fancy few would weave
    In these years! Yet, I feel,
If someone said on Christmas Eve,
    "Come; see the oxen kneel,

"In the lonely barton by yonder coomb
    Our childhood used to know,"
I should go with him in the gloom,
    Hoping it might be so.

Thomas Hardy

SIGHTS
and
SOUNDS

Upon Westminster Bridge

Earth has nothing to show more fair:
Dull would he be of soul who could pass by
A sight so touching in its majesty:
This City now doth, like a garment, wear
The beauty of the morning; silent, bare,
Ships, towers, domes, theatres, and temples lie
Open unto the fields, and to the sky;
All bright and glittering in the smokeless air.
Never did sun more beautifully steep
In his first splendour, valley, rock, or hill;
Ne'er saw I, never felt, a calm so deep!
The river glideth at his own sweet will:
Dear God! the very houses seem asleep;
And all that mighty heart is lying still!

William Wordsworth

On First Looking into Chapman's Homer

Much have I travell'd in the realms of gold,
　　And many goodly states and kingdoms seen;
　　Round many western islands have I been
Which bards in fealty to Apollo hold.
　　That deep-brow'd Homer ruled as his demesne;
　　Yet did I never breathe its pure serene
Till I heard Chapman speak out loud and bold:
Then felt I like some watcher of the skies
　　When a new planet swims into his ken;
Or like stout Cortez when with eagle eyes
　　He star'd at the Pacific – and all his men
Look'd at each other with a wild surmise –
　　Silent, upon a peak in Darien.

John Keats

149

Symphony in Yellow

An omnibus across the bridge
Crawls like a yellow butterfly,
And, here and there, a passer-by
Shows like a little restless midge.

Big barges full of yellow hay
Are moored against the shadowy wharf,
And, like a yellow silken scarf,
The thick fog hangs along the quay.

The yellow leaves begin to fade
And flutter from the Temple elms,
And at my feet the pale green Thames
Lies like a rod of rippled jade.

Oscar Wilde

A Thing of Beauty

A thing of beauty is a joy for ever:
Its loveliness increases; it will never
Pass into nothingness; but still will keep
A bower quiet for us, and a sleep
Full of sweet dreams, and health, and quiet breathing.
Therefore, on every morrow, are we wreathing
A flowery band to bind us to the earth,
Spite of despondence, of the inhuman death
Of noble natures, of the gloomy days,
Of all the unhealthy and o'er-darkened ways
Made for our searching: yes, in spite of all,
Some shape of beauty moves away the pall
From our dark spirits.

John Keats

From *The Garden*

What wondrous life in this I lead!
Ripe apples drop about my head;
The luscious clusters of the vine
Upon my mouth do crush their wine;
The nectarine, and curious peach,
Into my hands themselves do reach;
Stumbling on melons, as I pass,
Ensnared with flowers, I fall on grass.

Meanwhile the mind, from pleasure less,
Withdraws into its happiness:
The mind, that ocean where each kind
Does straight its own resemblance find;
Yet it creates, transcending these,
Far other worlds, and other seas;
Annihilating all that's made
To a green thought in a green shade.

Andrew Marvell

MUSIC
and
DANCING

Song's Eternity

What is song's eternity?
　　Come and see.
Can it noise and bustle be?
　　Come and see.
Praises sung or praises said
　　Can it be?
Wait awhile and these are dead –
　　Sigh – sigh;
Be they high or lowly bred
　　They die.

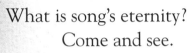

What is song's eternity?
　　Come and see.
Melodies of earth and sky,
　　Here they be.
Song once sung to Adam's ears
　　Can it be?
Ballads of six thousand years
　　Thrive, thrive;
Songs awaken with the spheres
　　Alive.

Mighty songs that miss decay,
　　What are they?
Crowds and cities pass away
　　Like a day.
Books are out and books are read;
　　What are they?
Years will lay them with the dead –
　　Sigh, sigh;
Trifles unto nothing wed,
　　They die.

Dreamers, mark the honey bee;
    Mark the tree
Where the blue cap "*tootle tee*"
    Sings a glee
Sung to Adam and to Eve –
    Here they be.
When floods covered every bough,
    Noah's ark
Heard that ballad singing now;
    Hark, hark,

"*Tootle tootle tootle tee*" –
    Can it be
Pride and fame must shadows be?
    Come and see –
Every season own her own;
    Bird and bee
Sing creation's music on;
    Nature's glee
Is in every mood and tone
    Eternity.

John Clare

155

Music

Orpheus with his lute made trees,
     And the mountain-tops that freeze,
Bow themselves when he did sing.
     To his music plants and flowers
Ever sprung: as sun and showers
     There had made a lasting spring.
Everything that heard him play,
     Even the billows of the sea,
Hung their heads, and then lay by.
     In sweet music is such art,
Killing care and grief of heart
     Fall asleep, or, hearing, die.

John Fletcher

Piano

Softly, in the dusk, a woman is singing to me;
Taking me back down the vista of years, till I see
A child sitting under the piano, in the boom of the tingling strings
And pressing the small, poised feet of a mother who smiles as she sings.

In spite of myself, the insidious mastery of song
Betrays me back, till the heart of me weeps to belong
To the old Sunday evenings at home, with winter outside
And hymns in the cosy parlour, the tinkling piano our guide.

So now it is vain for the singer to burst into clamour
With the great black piano appassionato. The glamour
Of childish days is upon me, my manhood is cast
Down in the flood of remembrance, I weep like a child for the past.

D. H. Lawrence

I Am of Ireland

I am of Ireland,
And of the holy land
Of Ireland.

Good sir, pray I thee,
For of saint charity,
Come and dance with me
In Ireland.

Anonymous

To Emilia V–

Music, when soft voices die,
Vibrates in the memory –
Odours, when sweet violets sicken,
Live within the sense they quicken.

Rose leaves, when the rose is dead,
Are heaped for the beloved's bed –
And so thy thoughts, when thou art gone,
Love itself shall slumber on…

Percy Bysshe Shelley

SADNESS
and
HAPPINESS

So, We'll Go No More A-Roving

So, we'll go no more a-roving
  So late into the night,
Though the heart be still as loving,
  And the moon be still as bright.

For the sword outwears its sheath,
  And the soul wears out the breast,
And the heart must pause to breathe,
  And love itself have rest.

Though the night was made for loving,
  And the day returns too soon,
Yet we'll go no more a-roving
  By the light of the moon.

George Gordon, Lord Byron

Spring and Fall

to a young child

Margaret, are you grieving
Over Goldengrove unleaving?
Leaves, like the things of man, you
With your fresh thoughts care for, can you?
Ah! as the heart grows older
It will come to such sights colder
By and by, nor spare a sigh
Though worlds of wanwood leafmeal lie,
And yet you *will* weep and know why.
Now no matter, child, the name:
Sorrow's springs are the same.
Nor mouth had, no nor mind, expressed
What heart heard of, ghost guessed:
It is the blight man was born for,
It is Margaret you mourn for.

Gerard Manley Hopkins

Canadian Boat Song

Listen to me, as when ye heard our father
Sing long ago the song of other shores –
Listen to me, and then in chorus gather
All your deep voices as ye pull your oars:
    Fair these broad meads – these hoary woods are grand
    But we are exiles from our fathers' land.

From the lone shieling of the misty island
Mountains divide us, and the waste of seas,
Yet still the blood is strong, the heart is Highland,
And we in dreams behold the Hebrides.

We ne'er shall tread the fancy-haunted valley,
Where 'tween the dark hills creeps the small clear stream,
In arms around the patriarch banner rally,
Nor see the moon on royal tombstones gleam.

When the bold kindred in the time long vanished,
Conquered the soil and fortified the keep –
No seer foretold the children would be banished,
That a degenerate lord might boast his sheep.

Come foreign rage – let Discord burst in slaughter!
O then for clansmen true, and stern claymore,
The hearts that would have given their blood like water,
Beat heavily beyond the Atlantic roar.
    Fair these broad meads – these hoary woods are grand
    But we are exiles from our fathers' land.

Anonymous

162

In the Highlands

In the highlands, in the country places,
Where the old plain men have rosy faces,
And the young fair maidens
Quiet eyes;
Where essential silence cheers and blesses,
And for ever in the hill-recesses
Her more lovely music
Broods and dies.

O to mount again where erst I haunted;
Where the old red hills are bird-enchanted,
And the low green meadows
Bright with sward;
And when even dies, the million-tinted,
And the night has come, and planets glinted,
Lo, the valley hollow
Lamp-bestarred!

O to dream, O to awake and wander
There, and with delight to take and render,
Through the trance of silence,
Quiet breath;
Lo! for there, among the flowers and grasses,
Only the mightier movement sounds and passes;
Only winds and rivers,
Life and death.

Robert Louis Stevenson

When in Disgrace With Fortune

When in disgrace with Fortune and men's eyes
I all alone beweep my outcast state,
And trouble deaf heaven with my bootless cries,
And look upon myself and curse my fate,
Wishing me like to one more rich in hope,
Featured like him, like him with friends possessed,
Desiring this man's art, and that man's scope,
With what I most enjoy contented least,
Yet in these thoughts myself almost despising,
Haply I think on thee, and then my state
(Like to the lark at break of day arising
From sullen earth) sings hymns at heaven's gate,
    For thy sweet love remembered such wealth brings,
    That then I scorn to change my state with kings.

William Shakespeare

Piping Down the Valleys Wild

Piping down the valleys wild,
Piping songs of pleasant glee,
On a cloud I saw a child,
And he laughing said to me:

"Pipe a song about a Lamb!"
So I piped with merry chear.
"Piper, pipe that song again;"
So I piped: he wept to hear.

"Drop thy pipe, thy happy pipe;
"Sing thy songs of happy chear:"
So I sung the same again,
While he wept with joy to hear.

"Piper, sit thee down and write
In a book, that all may read."
So he vanish'd from my sight,
And I pluck'd a hollow reed,

And I made a rural pen,
And I stain'd the water clear,
And I wrote my happy songs
Every child may joy to hear.

William Blake

A Lark's Nest

Now's the time for mirth and play,
Saturday's an holiday;
Praise to heav'n unceasing yield,
I've found a lark's nest in the field.

A lark's nest, then your play-mate begs
You'd spare herself and speckled eggs;
Soon she shall ascend and sing
Your praise to th'eternal King.

Christopher Smart

From *The Song of Solomon*

My beloved spake, and said unto me, Rise up, my love, my fair one,
and come away.
For lo, the winter is past, the rain is over, and gone.
The flowers appear on the earth, the time of the singing of birds is come,
and the voice of the turtle is heard in our land.
The fig tree putteth forth her green figs, and the vines with the tender
grape give a good smell.
Arise, my love, my fair one, and come away.

King James Bible

The Swing

How do you like to go up in a swing,
Up in the air so blue?
Oh, I do think it the pleasantest thing
Ever a child can do!

Up in the air and over the wall
Till I can see so wide,
Rivers and trees and cattle and all
Over the countryside –

Till I look down on the garden green,
Down on the roof so brown –
Up in the air I go flying again,
Up in the air and down!

Robert Louis Stevenson

Requiem

Under the wide and starry sky,
Dig the grave and let me lie.
Glad did I live and gladly die,
And I laid me down with a will.

This be the verse you grave for me:
Here he lies where he longed to be;
Home is the sailor, home from the sea,
And the hunter home from the hill.

Robert Louis Stevenson

SILLY
RHYMES

Elegy on the Death of a Mad Dog

Good people all, of every sort,
Give ear unto my song;
And if you find it wond'rous short,
It cannot hold you long.

In Islington there was a man,
Of whom the world might say,
That still a godly race he ran,
Whene'er he went to pray.

A kind and gentle heart he had,
To comfort friends and foes;
The naked every day he clad,
When he put on his clothes.

And in that town a dog was found,
As many dogs there be,
Both mongrel, puppy, whelp, and hound,
And curs of low degree.

This dog and man at first were friends;
But when a pique began,
The dog, to gain some private ends,
Went mad and bit the man.

Around from all the neighbouring streets
The wond'ring neighbours ran,
And swore the dog had lost its wits,
To bite so good a man.

The wound it seem'd both sore and sad
To every Christian eye;
And while they swore the dog was mad,
They swore the man would die.

But soon a wonder came to light,
That showed the rogues they lied:
The man recover'd of the bite,
The dog it was that died.

Oliver Goldsmith

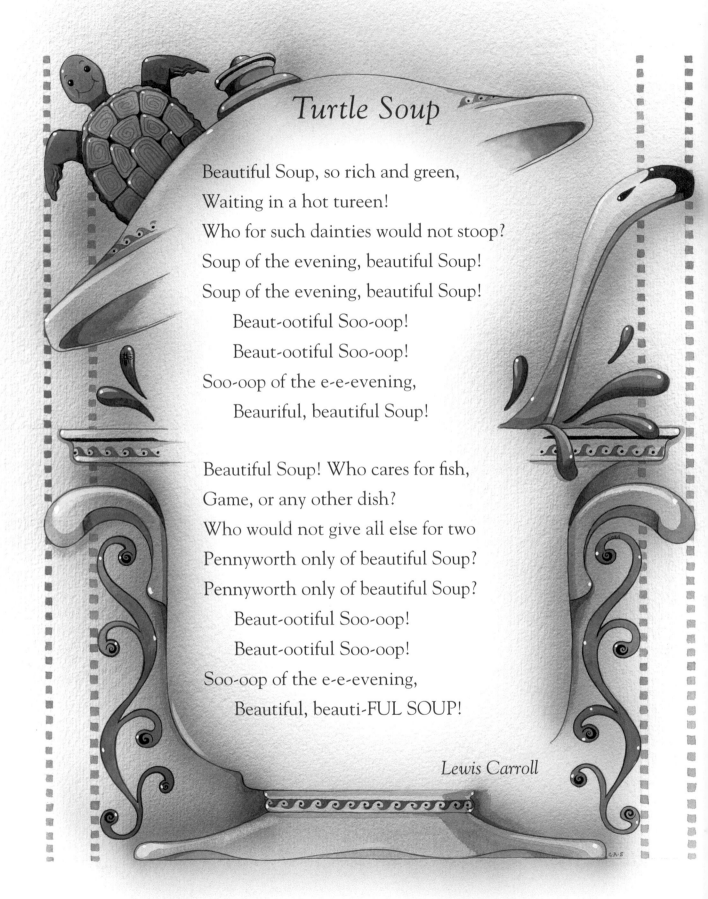

Turtle Soup

Beautiful Soup, so rich and green,
Waiting in a hot tureen!
Who for such dainties would not stoop?
Soup of the evening, beautiful Soup!
Soup of the evening, beautiful Soup!
    Beaut-ootiful Soo-oop!
    Beaut-ootiful Soo-oop!
Soo-oop of the e-e-evening,
    Beauriful, beautiful Soup!

Beautiful Soup! Who cares for fish,
Game, or any other dish?
Who would not give all else for two
Pennyworth only of beautiful Soup?
Pennyworth only of beautiful Soup?
    Beaut-ootiful Soo-oop!
    Beaut-ootiful Soo-oop!
Soo-oop of the e-e-evening,
    Beautiful, beauti-FUL SOUP!

Lewis Carroll

There was an Old Man with a Beard

There was an Old Man with a beard,
Who said, it is just as I feared!
   Two Owls and a Hen,
    Four Larks and a Wren,
Have all built their nests in my beard!

Edward Lear

The Reverend Henry Ward Beecher

The Reverend Henry Ward Beecher
Called a hen a most elegant creature
   The hen, pleased with that,
    Laid an egg in his hat,
And thus did the hen reward Beecher.

Edward Lear

175

The Mad Hatter's Song

Twinkle, twinkle, little bat!
How I wonder what you're at!
Up above the world you fly,
Like a tea-tray in the sky.
Twinkle, twinkle…

Lewis Carroll

There was an Old Man…

There was an Old Man in a tree,
Who was horribly bored by a Bee;
   When they said, "Does it buzz?"
   He replied, "Yes, it does!"
"It's a regular brute of a Bee!"

Lewis Carroll

There was an Old Man with a flute,
A sarpint ran into his boot;
But he played day and night,
Till the sarpint took flight,
And avoided that man with a flute.

Lewis Carroll

176

Calico Pie

Calico Pie,
The little Birds fly
Down to the calico tree,
Their wings were blue,
And they sang "Tilly-loo!"
Till away they flew,
And they never came back to me!
They never came back!
They never came back!
They never came back to me!

Calico Jam,
The little Fish swam,
Over the syllabub sea,
He took off his hat,
To the Sole and the Sprat,
And the Willeby-wat,
But he never came back to me!
He never came back!
He never came back!
He never came back to me!

Calico Ban,

The little Mice ran,

To be ready in time for tea,

Flippity flup,

They drank it all up,

And danced in the cup,

But they never came back to me!

They never came back!

They never came back!

They never came back to me!

Calico Drum,

The Grasshoppers come,

The Butterfly, Beetle, and Bee,

Over the ground,

Around and round,

With a hop and a bound,

And they never came back to me!

They never came back!

They never came back!

They never came back to me!

Edward Lear

Little Birds

Little Birds are dining
　　Warily and well
　　　Hid in mossy cell:
Hid, I say, by waiters
Gorgeous in their gaiters –
　　　I've a Tale to tell.

Little Birds are feeding
　　Justices with jam,
　　　Rich in frizzled ham:
Rich, I say, in oysters –
Haunting shady cloisters –
　　　That is what I am.

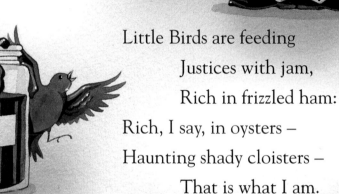

Little Birds are teaching
　　Tigresses to smile,
　　　Innocent of guile:
Smile, I say, not smirkle –
Mouth a semicircle,
　　　That's the proper style!

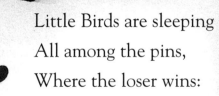

Little Birds are sleeping
　　All among the pins,
　　　Where the loser wins:
Where, I say, he sneezes,
When and how he pleases –
　　　So the Tale begins.

179

Little Birds are writing
    Interesting books,
      To be read by cooks;
Read, I say, not roasted –
Letterpress, when toasted,
      Loses its good looks.

Little Birds are seeking,
    Hecatombs of haws,
      Dressed in snowy gauze:
Dressed, I say, in fringes
Half-alive with hinges –
      Thus they break the laws.

Little Birds are playing
    Bagpipes on the shore,
      Where the tourists snore:
"Thanks!" they cry. "'Tis thrilling.
Take, oh, take this shilling!
      Let us have no more!"

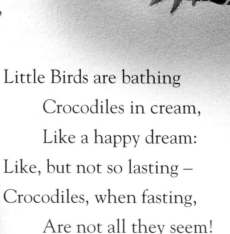

Little Birds are bathing
    Crocodiles in cream,
      Like a happy dream:
Like, but not so lasting –
Crocodiles, when fasting,
      Are not all they seem!

Little Birds are choking
      Baronets with bun,
      Taught to fire a gun:
Taught, I say, to splinter
Salmon in the winter –
      Merely for the fun.

Little Birds are hiding
      Crimes in carpet-bags,
      Blessed by happy stags:
Blessed, I say, though beaten –
Since our friends are eaten
      When the memory flags.

Little Birds are tasting
      Gratitude and gold,
      Pale with sudden cold;
Pale, I say, and wrinkled –
When the bells have tinkled,
      And the Tale is told.

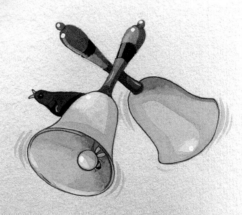

Lewis Carroll

The White Knight's Song

I'll tell thee everything I can;
    There's little to relate,
I saw an aged aged man,
    A-sitting on a gate.
"Who are you, aged man?" I said.
    "And how is it you live?"
And his answer trickled through my head
    Like water through a sieve.

He said "I look for butterflies
    That sleep among the wheat:
I make them into mutton-pies,
    And sell them in the street.
I sell them unto men," he said,
    "Who sail on stormy seas;
And that's the way I get my bread –
    A trifle, if you please."

But I was thinking of a plan
    To dye one's whiskers green,
And always use so large a fan
    That they could not be seen.
So, having no reply to give
    To what the old man said,
I cried, "Come, tell me how you live!"
    And thumped him on the head.

His accents mild took up the tale:
　　He said "I go my ways,
And when I find a mountain-rill,
　　I set it in a blaze;
And thence they make a stuff they call
　　Rowland's Macassar-Oil –
Yet twopence-halfpenny is all
　　They give me for my toil."

But I was thinking of a way
　　To feed oneself on batter,
And so go on from day to day
　　Getting a little fatter.
I shook him well from side to side,
　　Until his face was blue:
"Come, tell me how you live," I cried,
　　"And what it is you do!"

He said "I hunt for haddocks' eues
　　Among the heather bright,
And work them into waistcoat-buttons
　　In the silent night.
And these I do not sell for gold
　　Or coin of silvery shine,
But for a copper halfpenny,
　　And that will purchase nine.

"I sometimes dig for buttered rolls,
        Or set limed twigs for crabs;
I sometimes search the grassy knolls
        For wheels of Hansom-cabs.
And that's the way" (he gave a wink)
        "By which I get my wealth –
And very gladly will I drink
        Your Honour's noble health."

I heard him then, for I had just
        Completed my design
To keep the Menai bridge from rust
        By boiling it in wine.
I thanked him much for telling me
        The way he got his wealth,
But chiefly for his wish that he
        Might drink my noble health.

And now, if e'er by chance I put
        My fingers into glue,
Or madly squeeze a right-hand foot
        Into a left-hand shoe,
Or if I drop upon my toe
        A very heavy weight,
I weep, for it reminds me so
Of that old man I used to know –

Whose look was mild, whose speech was slow,
Whose hair was whiter than the snow,
Whose face was very like a crow,
With eyes, like cinders, all aglow,
Who seemed distracted with his woe,
Who rocked his body to and fro,
And muttered mumblingly and low,
As if his mouth were full of dough,
Who snorted like a buffalo –
That summer evening long ago
        A-sitting on a gate.

Lewis Carroll

Incidents in the Life of my Uncle Arly

O my aged Uncle Arly!
Sitting on a heap of Barley
Thro' the silent hours of night,
Close beside a leafy thicket:
On his nose there was a Cricket,
In his hat a Railway-Ticket;
(But his shoes were far too tight.)

Long ago, in youth, he squander'd
All his goods away, and wander'd
To the Tiniskoop-hills afar.
There on golden sunsets blazing,
Every evening found him gazing,
Singing, – "Orb! you're quite amazing!
How I wonder what you are!"

Like the ancient Medes and Persians,
Always by his own exertions
He subsisted on those hills;
Whiles, – by teaching children spelling,
Or at times by merely yelling,
Or at intervals by selling
Propter's Nicodemus Pills.

Later, in his morning rambles
He perceived the moving brambles –
Something square and white disclose;
'Twas a First-class Railway-Ticket,
But, on stooping down to pick it
Off the ground, – a pea-green Cricket
Settled on my uncle's Nose.

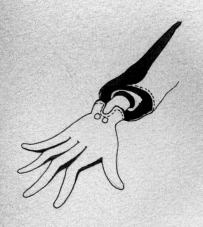

Never – never more, – oh! never,
Did that Cricket leave him ever,
Dawn or evening, day or night;
Clinging as a constant treasure,
Chirping with a cheerious measure,
Wholly to my uncle's pleasure,
(Though his shoes were far too tight.)

So for three-and-forty winters,
Till his shoes were worn to splinters,
All those hills he wander'd o'er,
Sometimes silent; – sometimes yelling;
Till he came to Borley-Melling,
Near his old ancestral dwelling;
(But his shoes were far too tight.)

On a little heap of Barley
Died my aged uncle Arly,
And they buried him one night;
Close beside the leafy thicket;
There, – his hat and Railway-Ticket;
There, – his ever-faithful Cricket;
(But his shoes were far too tight.)

Edward Lear

The Mad Gardener's Song

He thought he saw an Elephant,
    That practised on a fife:
He looked again, and found it was
    A letter from his wife.
"At length I realise," he said,
    "The bitterness of Life!"

He thought he saw a Buffalo
    Upon the chimney-piece:
He looked again, and found it was
    His Sister's Husband's Niece.
"Unless you leave this house," he said,
    "I'll send for the Police!"

He thought he saw a Rattlesnake
    That questioned him in Greek:
He looked again, and found it was
    The Middle of Next Week.
"The only thing I regret," he said,
    "Is that it cannot speak!"

He thought he saw a Banker's Clerk
    Descending from the bus:
He looked again, and found it was
    A Hippopotamus:
"If this should stay to dine," he said,
    "There won't be much for us!"

He thought he saw a Kangaroo
    That worked a coffee-mill:
He looked again, and found it was
    A Vegetable-Pill.
"Were I to swallow this," he said,
    "I should be very ill!"

He thought he saw a Coach-and-Four
    That stood beside his bed:
He looked again, and found it was
    A bear without a Head.
"Poor thing," he said, "poor silly thing!
    It's waiting to be fed!"

He thought he saw an Albatross
        That fluttered round the lamp:
He looked again, and found it was
        A Penny-Postage-Stamp.
"You'd best be getting home," he said:
        "The nights are very damp!"

He thought he saw a Garden-Door
        That opened with a key:
He looked again, and found it was
        A Double Rule of Three:
"And all its mystery," he said,
        "Is clear as day to me!"

He thought he saw an Argument
        That proved he was the Pope:
He looked again, and found it was
        A Bar of Mottled Soap.
"A fact so dread," he faintly said,
        "Extinguishes all hope!"

Lewis Carroll

The Akond of Swat

Who, or why, or which, or what, Is the Akond of SWAT?

Is he tall or short, or dark or fair?

Does he sit on a stool or sofa or chair,   or SQUAT,
                              The Akond of Swat?

Is he wise or foolish, young or old?

Does he drink his soup and his coffee cold,   or HOT,
                              The Akond of Swat?

Does he sing or whistle, jabber or talk,

And when riding abroad does he gallop or walk,   or TROT,
                              The Akond of Swat?

Does he wear a turban, a fez or a hat?

Does he sleep on a mattress, a bed or a mat,   or a COT,
                              The Akond of Swat?

When he writes a copy in round-hand size,

Does he cross his T's and finish his I's   with a DOT,
                              The Akond of Swat?

Can he write a letter concisely clear,

Without a speck or a smudge or smear   or BLOT,
                              The Akond of Swat?

Do his people like him extremely well?

Or do they, whenever they can, rebel,
                                                    or PLOT,
                                At the Akond of Swat?

If he catches them then, either old or young,

Does he have them chopped in pieces or hung,
                                                    or SHOT,
                                The Akond of Swat?

Do his people prig in the lanes or park?

Or even at times, when days are dark,
                                                    GAROTTE?
                                O the Akond of Swat?

Does he study the wants of his own dominion?

Or doesn't he care for public opinion
                                                    a JOT,
                                The Akond of Swat?

To amuse his mind do his people show him

Pictures, or anyone's last new poem,
                                                    or WHAT,
                                For the Akond of Swat?

At night if he suddenly screams and wakes,

Do they bring him only a few small cakes,
                                                    or a LOT,
                                For the Akond of Swat?

Does he live on turnips, tea or tripe,

Does he like his shawl to be marked with a stripe,
                                                    or a DOT,
                                The Akond of Swat?

Does he like to lie on his back in a boat
Like the lady who lived that isle remote, SHALLOT,
The Akond of Swat?

Is he quiet, or always making a fuss?
Is his steward a Swiss or a Swede or a Russ, or a SCOT,
The Akond of Swat?

Does he like to sit by the calm blue wave?
Or to sleep and snore in a dark green cave, or a GROTT,
The Akond of Swat?

Does he drink small beer from a silver jug?
Or a bowl? or a glass? or a cup? or a mug? or a POT,
The Akond of Swat?

Does he wear a white tie when he dines with his friends,
And tie it neat in a abow with ends, or a KNOT,
The Akond of Swat?

Does he like new cream, and hate mince-pies?
When he looks at the sun does he wink his eyes, or NOT,
The Akond of Swat?

Does he teach his subjects to roast and bake?
Does he sail about on an inland lake, in a YACHT,
The Akond of Swat?

Some one, or nobody knows I wot
Who or which or why or what

Is The Akond of Swat!

Edward Lear

NEARLY
NONSENSE

There was an old loony of Lyme,
Whose candour was simply sublime;
    When they asked, "Are you there?"
    "Yes," he said, "but take care,
For I'm never 'all there' at a time".

Anonymous

There was a young lady of Ryde,
Who ate some green apples and died.
    The apples fermented
    Inside the lamented,
And made cider inside her inside.

Anonymous

There was an old man of Dunoon
Who always ate soup with a fork.
For he said: "As I eat
Neither fish, fowl, nor flesh,
I should otherwise finish too quick."

Anonymous

There was an Old Person of Slough,
Who danced at the end of a Bough;
But they said, "If you sneeze,
You might damage the trees,
You imprudent Old Person of Slough."

Edward Lear

There was an Old Person in Gray,
Whose feelings were tinged with dismay;
She purchased two Parrots,
And fed them with Carrots,
Which pleased that Old Person in Gray.

Edward Lear

199

There was once a young man of Oporta
Who daily got shorter and shorter,
	The reason he said
	Was the hod on his head,
Which was filled with the heaviest mortar.

His sister named Lucy O'Finner,
Grew constantly thinner and thinner,
	The reason was plain,
	She slept out in the rain,
And was never allowed any dinner.

Lewis Carroll

There was an Old Person of Anerly,
Whose conduct was strange and unmannerly;
    He rushed down the Strand,
    With a Pig in each hand,
But returned in the evening to Anerley.

Edward Lear

There was a Young Lady of Welling,
Whose praise all the world was a telling;
    She played on the harp,
    And caught several carp,
That accomplished Young Lady of Welling.

Edward Lear

There was a Young Girl of Majorca,
Whose aunt was a very fast walker;
    She walked seventy miles,
    And leaped fifteen stiles,
Which astonished that Girl of Majorca.

Edward Lear

The Great Panjandrum

So she went into the garden
to cut a cabbage-leaf
to make an apple-pie,
and at the same time
a great she-bear, coming down the street,
pops its head into the shop.
What! no soap?
            So he died,
and she very imprudently married the Barber:
and there were present
the Picninnies,
            and the Joblillies,
                and the Garyulies,
and the great Panjandrum himself,
with the little round button at top;
and they all fell to playing the game of catch-as-catch-can,
till the gunpowder ran out at the heels of their boots.

Samuel Foote

A Quadrupedremian Song

He dreamt that he saw the Buffalant,
And the spottified Dromedaraffe,
The blue Camelotamus, lean and gaunt,
And the wild Tigeroceros calf.

The maned Liodillo loudly roared,
And the Peccarbok whistled its whine,
The Chinchayak leapt on the dewy sward,
As it hunted the pale Baboopine.

He dreamt that he met the Crocoghau,
As it swam in the Stagnolent Lake;
But everything that in dreams he saw
Came of eating too freely of cake.

Thomas Wood

The Duck and the Kangaroo

Said the Duck to the Kangaroo,
    "Good gracious! how you hop!
Over the fields and the water too,
    As if you never would stop!
My life is a bore in this nasty pond,
And I long to go out in the world beyond!
    I wish I could hop like you!"
    Said the Duck to the Kangaroo.

"Please give me a ride on your back!"
    Said the Duck to the Kangaroo.
"I would sit quite still, and say nothing but 'Quack,'
    The whole of the long day through!
And we'd go to the Dee, and the Jelly Bo Lee,
Over the land, and over the sea;
    Please take me a ride! O do!"
    Said the Duck to the Kangaroo.

Said the Kangaroo to the Duck,
    "This requires some little reflection;
Perhaps on the whole it might bring me luck,
    And there seems but one objection,
Which is, if you'll let me speak so bold,
Your feet are unpleasantly wet and cold,
And would probably give me the roo –
    Matiz!" said the Kangaroo.

Said the Duck, "As I sat on the rocks,
     I have thought over that completely,
And I bought four pairs of worsted socks
     Which fit my web-feet neatly.
And to keep out the cold I've bought a cloak,
And every day a cigar I'll smoke,
     All to follow my own dear true
     Love of a Kangaroo!"

Said the Kangaroo, "I'm ready!
     All in the moonlight pale;
But to balance me well, dear Duck, sit steady!
     And quite at the end of my tail!"
So away they went with a hop and a bound,
And they hopped the whole world three times round;
     And who so happy, – O who,
     As the Duck and the Kangaroo?

Edward Lear

To Marie

When the breeze from the bluebottle's blustering blim
Twirls the toads in a tooramaloo,
And the whiskery whine of the wheedlesome whim
Drowns the roll of the rattatattoo,
Then I dream in the shade of the shally-g-shee,
And the voice of the bally-molay
Brings the smell of the pale poppy-cod's blummered blee
From the willy-wad over the way.

Ah, the shuddering shoe and the blinketty-blanks
When the punglung falls from the bough
In the blast of a hurricane's hicketty-hanks
O'er the hills of the hocketty-how!
Give the rigamarole to the clangery-whang,
If they care for such fiddlededee;
But the thingumbob kiss of the whangery-bang
Keeps the higgledy-piggle for me.

Anonymous

206

L'Envoi

It is pilly-po-doddle and aligobung
When the lollypup covers the ground,
Yet the poldiddle perishes plunkety-pung
When the heart jimny-coggles around.
If the soul cannot snoop at the gigglesome cart
Seeking surcease in gluggety-glug,
It is useless to say to the pulsating heart,
"Yankee-doodle ker-chuggety-chug!"

Anonymous

207

I Saw a Peacock

I saw a peacock with a fiery tail
I saw a blazing comet pour down hail
I saw a cloud all wrapt with ivy round
I saw a lofty oak creep on the ground
I saw a beetle swallow up a whale
I saw a foaming sea brimful of ale
I saw a pewter cup sixteen feet deep
I saw a well full of men's tears that weep
I saw wet eyes in flames of living fire
I saw a house as high as the moon and higher
I saw the glorious sun at deep midnight
I saw the man who saw this wondrous sight.

I saw a fishpond all on fire
I saw a houe bow to a squire
I saw a parson twelve feet high
I saw a cottage near the sky
I saw a balloon made of lead
I saw a coffin drop down dead
I saw a sparrow run a race
I saw two horses making lace
I saw a girl just like a cat
I saw a kitten wear a hat
I saw a man who saw these too,
And say, though strange, they all are true.

Anonymous

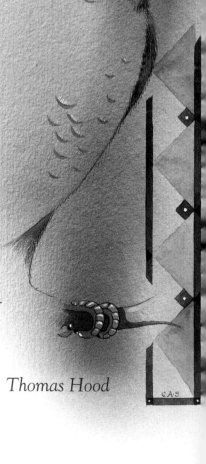

Muddled Metaphors

Oh, ever thus from childhood's hour
I've seen my fondest hopes recede!
I never loved a tree or flower
That didn't trump its partner's lead.

I never nursed a dear gazelle,
To glad me with its dappled hide,
But when it came to know me well
It fell upon the buttered side.

I never taught a cockatoo
To whistle comic songs profound,
But just when "Jolly Dogs" it knew
It failed for ninepence in the pound.

I never reared a walrus cub
In my aquarium to plunge,
But, when it learnt to love its tub,
It placidly threw up the sponge.

I never strove a metaphor
To every bosom home to bring,
But – just as it had reached the door –
It went and cut a pigeon's wing.

Thomas Hood

210

RHYMES
without
REASON

The Jumblies

They went to sea in a Sieve, they did,
    In a Sieve they went to sea:
In spite of all their friends could say,
On a winter's morn, on a stormy day,
    In a Sieve they went to sea!
And when the Sieve turned round and round,
And everyone cried, 'You'll all be drowned!"
They called aloud, "Our Sieve ain't big,
But we don't care a button! we don't care a fig!
    In a Sieve we'll go to sea!"
        Far and few, far and few,
        Are the lands where the Jumblies live;
        Their heads are green, and their hands are blue,
        And they went to sea in a Sieve.

They sailed in a Sieve, they did,
　　In a Sieve they sailed so fast,
With only a beautiful pea-green veil
Tied with a riband by way of a sail,
　　To a small tobacco-pipe mast;
And every one said, who saw them go,
"O won't they be soon upset, you know!
For the sky is darm, and the voyage is long,
And happen what may, it's extremely wrong
　　In a Sieve to sail so fast!"
　　　　Far and few, far and few,
　　　　Are the lands where the Jumblies live;
　　　　Their heads are green, and their hands are blue,
　　　　And they went to sea in a Sieve.

The water it soon came in, it did,
　　The water it soon came in;
So to keep them dry, they wrapped their feet
In a pinky paper all folded near,
　　And they fastened it down with a pin.
And they passed the night in a crockery-jar,
And each of them said, "How wise we are!
Though the sky be dark, and the voyage be long,
Yet we never can think we were rash or wrong,
　　While round in our Sieve we spin!"
　　　　Far and few, far and few,
　　　　Are the lands where the Jumblies live;
　　　　Their heads are green, and their hands are blue,
　　　　And they went to sea in a Sieve.

213

And all night long they sailed away;
    And when the sun went down,
They whistled and warbled a moony song
To the echoing sound of a coppry gong,
    In the shade of the mountains brown.
"O Timballo! How happy we are,
When we live in a sieve and a crockery-jar,
And all night long in the moonlight pale,
We sail away with a pea-green sail,
    In the shade of the mountains brown!"
      Far and few, far and few,
      Are the lands where the Jumblies live;
      Their heads are green, and their hands are blue,
      And they went to sea in a Sieve.

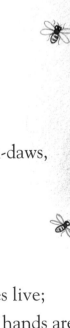

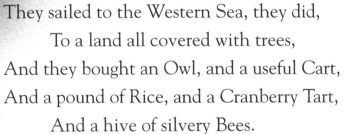

They sailed to the Western Sea, they did,
    To a land all covered with trees,
And they bought an Owl, and a useful Cart,
And a pound of Rice, and a Cranberry Tart,
    And a hive of silvery Bees.
And they bought a Pig, and some green Jack-daws,
And a lovely Monkey with lollipop paws,
And forty bottles of Ring-Bo-ree,
    And no end of Stilton Cheese.
      Far and few, far and few,
      Are the lands where the Jumblies live;
      Their heads are green, and their hands are blue,
      And they went to sea in a Sieve.

And in twenty years they all came back,
     In twenty years or more,
And everyone said, "How tall they've grown!
For they've been to the Lakes, and the Torrible Zone,
     And the hill of the Chankly Bore";
And they drank their health, and gave them a feast
Of dumplings made of beautiful yeast;
And every one said, "If we only live,
We too will go to sea in a Sieve,
     To the hills of the Chankly Bore!"
          Far and few, far and few,
          Are the lands where the Jumblies live;
          Their heads are green, and their hands are blue,
          And they went to sea in a Sieve.

Edward Lear

The Sugar-Plum Tree

Have you ever heard of the Sugar-Plum Tree?
'Tis a marvel of great renown!
It blooms on the shore of the Lollipop Sea
In the garden of Shut-Eye Town;
The fruit that it bears is so wondrously sweet
(As those who have tasted it say)
That good little children have only to eat
Of that fruit to be happy next day.

When you've got to the tree, you would have a hard time
To capture the fruit which I sing;
The tree is so tall that no person could climb
To the boughs where the sugar-plums swing!
But up in that tree sits a chocolate cat,
And a gingerbread dog prowls below –
And this is the way you contrive to get at
Those sugar-plums tempting you so:

You say but the word to that gingerbread dog
And he barks with such terrible zest
That the chocolate cat is at once all agog,
As her swelling proportions attest.

And the chocolate cat goes cavorting around
From this leafy limb unto that,
And the sugar-plums tumble, of course, to the ground –
Hurrah for that chocolate cat!

There are marshmallows, gumdrops, and peppermint canes,
With stripings of scarlet or gold,
And you carry away of the treasure that rains
As much as your apron can hold!
So come, little child, cuddle closer to me
In your dainty white nightcap and gown,
And I'll rock you away to that Sugar-Plum Tree
In the garden of Shut-Eye Town.

Eugene Field

Skipping Rhymes

Piggy on the railway, picking up the stones
Up came an engine, and broke Piggy's bones.
"Oh," said Piggy, "that's not fair!"
"Oh," said the driver, "I don't care!"

Buster Brown went to town
With his pants on upside down.
He lost a nickel,
He bought a pickle.
The pickle was sour,
He bought a flower.
The flower was yellow,
He met a fellow.
The fellow was mean,
He bought a bean.
The bean was hard,
He bought a card.
And on the card
It said, "Red hot pepper!"

Doctor Brown fell in the well,
Broke his collar bone.
Why don't he tend to the sick,
And leave the well alone?

Tarzan, Tarzan, in the air,
Tarzan lost his underwear.
Tarzan say, "Me no care,
Jane make me another pair."
Jane, Jane, in the air,
Jane lost her underwear.
Jane say, "Me no care,
Cheetah make me another pair."
Cheetah, Cheetah, in the air,
Cheetah lost his underwear.
Cheetah say, "Me no care,
Cheetah need no underwear."

Obediah jumped in the fire.
Fire so hot, jumped in a pot.
Pot so little, jumped in a kettle.
Kettle so black, jumped in a crack.
Crack so high, jumped to the sky.
Sky so blue, jumped in a canoe.
Canoe so shallow, jumped the tallow.
Tallow so hard, jumped in the lard.
Lard so soft, jumped in the loft.
Loft so rotten, fell in the cotton.
Cotton so white, he stayed all night.

The Dong With a Luminous Nose

When awful darkness and silence reign
Over the great Gromboolian plain,
    Through the long, long wintry nights;
When the angry breakers roar
As they beat on the rocky shore;
    When Storm-clouds brood on the towering heights
Of the Hills of the Chankly Bore:

Then, throught the vast and gloomy dark,
There moves what seems a fiery spark,
    A lonely spark with silvery rays
    Piercing the coal-black night,
    A Meteor strange and bright:
Hither and thither the vision strays,
A single lurid light.

Slowly it wanders, – pauses, – creeps,
Anon it sparkes, – flashes and leaps;
And ever onward it gleaming goes
A light on the Bong-tree stems it throws.
And those who watch at that midnight hour
From Hall or Terrace, or lofty Tower,
Cry, as the wild light passes along,
    "The Dong! – the Dong!
"The wandering Dong through the forest goes!
    "The Dong! the Dong!
"The Dong with a luminous Nose!"

Long years ago
The Dong was happy and gay,
Till he fell in love with a Jumbly Girl
Who came to those shores one day,
For the Jumblies came in a sieve, they did –
Landing at even near the Zemmery Fidd
Where the Oblong Oysters grow,
And the rocks are smooth and gray.
And all the woods and the valleys rang
With the Chorus they daily and nightly sang,
"Far and few, far and few,
Are the lands where the Jumblies live;
Their heads are green, and their hands are blue
And they went to sea in a sieve."

221

Happily, happily passed those days!
      While the cheerful Jumblies staid;
  They danced in circlets all night long,
  To the plaintive pipe of the lively Dong,
      In moonlight, shine, or shade.
For day and night he was always there
By the side of the Jumbly Girl so fair,
With her sky-blue hands, and her sea-green hair.
Till the morning came of that hateful day
When the Jumblies sailed in their sieve away,
And the Dong was left on the cruel shore
Gazing – gazing for evermore,
Ever keeping his weary eyes on
That pea-green sail on the far horizon,
Singing the Jumbly Chorus still
As he sat all day on the grassy hill,
      "Far and few, far and few,
      Are the lands where the Jumblies live;
      Their heads are green, and their hands are blue
      And they went to sea in a sieve."

But when the sun was low in the West,
    The Dong arose and said;
      "What little sense I once possessed
      Has quite gone out of my head!"
And since that day he wanders still
By lake and forest, marsh and hill,
Singing – "O somewhere, in valley or plain
"Might I find my Jumbly Girl again!
"For ever I'll seek by lake and shore
"Till I find my Jumbly Girl once more!"

Playing a pipe with silvery squeaks,
Since then his Jumbly Girl he seeks,
And because by night he could not see,
He gathered the bark of the Twangum Tree
    On the flowery plain that grows.
    And he wove him a wondrous Nose,
A Nose as strange as a Nose could be!
Of vast proportions and painted red,
And tied with cords to the back of his head.
    – In a hollow rounded space it ended
    With a luminous Lamp within suspended,
      All fenced about
      With a bandage stout
      To prevent the wind from blowing it out;
And with holes all round to send the light,
In gleaming rays on the dismal night.

223

And now each night, and all night long,
Over those plains still roams the Dong;
And above the wail of the Chimp and Snipe
You may hear the squeak of his plaintive pipe
While ever he seeks, but seeks in vain
To meet with his Jumbly Girl again;
Lonely and wild – all night he goes,
The Dong with a luminous Nose!
And all who watch at the midnight hour,
From Hall or Terrace, or lofty Tower,
Cry, as they trace the Meteor bright,
Moving along through the dreary night,

   "This is the hour when forth he goes,
   "The Dong with a luminous Nose!
   "Yonder – over the plain he goes;
    "He goes!
    "He goes;
   "The Dong with a luminous Nose!"

Edward Lear

224

SILLY
STORIES

Sally Simpkin's Lament *or* John Jones's Kit-Cat-astrophe

"Oh! what is that comes gliding in,
And quite in middling haste?
It is the picture of my Jones,
And painted to the waist.

"It is not painted to the life,
For where's the trowsers blue?
Oh Jones, my dear! – Oh dear! my Jones,
What is become of you?"

"Oh! Sally dear, it is too true,
The half that you remark
Is come to say my other half
Is bit off by a shark!

"Oh! Sally, sharks do things by halves,
Yet most completely do!
A bite in one place seems enough,
But I've been bit in two.

"You know I once was all your own,
But now a shark must share!
But let that pass – for now to you
I'm neither here nor there.

"Alas! death has a strange divorce
Effected in the sea,
It has divided me from you,
And even me from me!

"Don't fear my ghost will walk 'o nights
To haunt as people say;
My ghost can't walk, for, oh! my legs
Are many leagues away!

"Lord! think when I am swimming round,
And looking where the boat is,
A shark just snaps away a half,
Without 'a quarter's notice'.

"One half is here, the other half
Is near Columbia placed;
Oh! Sally, I have got the whole
Atlantic for my waist.

"But now, adieu – a long adieu!
I've solved death's awful riddle,
And would say more, but I am doomed
To break off in the middle."

Thomas Hood

The Walrus and the Carpenter

The sun was shining on the sea
Shining with all his might:
He did his very best to make
The billows smooth and bright –
And this was odd, because it was
The middle of the night.

The moon was shining sulkily,
Because she thought the sun
Had got no business to be there
After the day was done –
"It's very rude of him," she said,
"To come and spoil the fun!"

The sea was wet as wet could be,
The sands were dry as dry.
You could not see a cloud, because
No cloud was in the sky:
No birds were flying overhead –
There were no birds to fly.

The Walrus and the Carpenter
Were walking close at hand;
They wept like anything to see
Such quantities of sand:
"If this were only cleared away,"
They said, "it would be grand!"

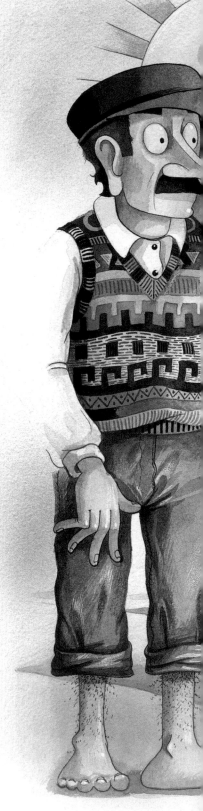

"If seven maids with seven mops
Swept it for half a year,
Do you suppose," the Walrus said,
"That they could get it clear?"
"I doubt it," said the Carpenter,
And shed a bitter tear.

"O Oysters, come and walk with us!"
The Walrus did beseech.
"A pleasant walk, a pleasant talk,
Along the briny beach:
We cannot do with more than four,
To give a hand to each."

The eldest Oyster looked at him,
But never a word he said:
The eldest Oyster winked his eye,
And shook his heavy head –
Meaning to say he did not choose
To leave the oyster-bed.

But four young Oysters hurried up,
All eager for the treat:
Their coats were brushed, their faces washed,
Their shoes were clean and neat –
And this was odd, because, you know,
They hadn't any feet.

Four other Oysters followed them,
And yet another four;
And thick and fast they came at last,
And more, and more, and more –
All hopping through the frothy waves,
And scrambling to the shore.

The Walrus and the Carpenter
Walked on a mile or so.
And then they rested on a rock
Conveniently low:
And all the little Oysters stood
And waited in a row.

"The time has come," the Walrus said,
"To talk of many things:
Of shoes – sand ships – and sealing-wax –
Of cabbages – and kings –
And why the sea is boiling hot –
And whether pigs have wings."

"But wait a bit," the Oysters cried,
"Before we have our chat;
For some of us are out of breath,
And all of us are fat!"
"No hurry!" said the Carpenter.
They thanked him much for that.

"A loaf of bread," the Walrus said,
"Is what we chiefly need:
Pepper and vinegar besides
Are very good indeed –
Now if you're ready, Oysters dear,
We can begin to feed."

"But not on us!" the Oysters cried,
Turning a little blue.
"After such kindness, that would be
A dismal thing to do!"
"The night is fine," the Walrus said,
"Do you admire the view?"

"It was so kind of you to come!
And you are very nice!"
The Carpenter said nothing but
"Cut us another slice:
I wish you were not quite so deaf –
I've had to ask you twice!"

"It seems a shame," the Walrus said,
"To play them such a trick,
After we've brought them out so far,
And made them trot so quick!"
The Carpenter said nothing but
"The butter's spread too thick!"

"I weep for you," the Walrus said:
"I deeply sympathize."
With sobs and tears he sorted out
Those of the largest size,
Holding his pocket-handkerchief
Before his streaming eyes.

"O Oysters," said the Carpenter,
"You've had a pleasant run!
Shall we be trotting home again?"
But answer came there none –
And this was scarcely odd, because
They'd eaten every one.

Lewis Carroll

Simple Simon

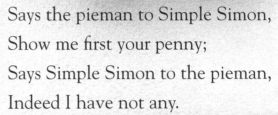

Simple Simon met a pieman
Going to the fair;
Says Simple Simon to the pieman,
Let me taste your ware.

Says the pieman to Simple Simon,
Show me first your penny;
Says Simple Simon to the pieman,
Indeed I have not any.

Simple Simon went a-fishing,
For to catch a whale;
All the water he had got
Was in his mother's pail.

Simple Simon went a-hunting,
For to catch a hare;
He rode a goat about the streets,
But couldn't find one there.

He went to catch a dickey bird,
And thought he could not fail,
Because he'd got a little salt
To put upon its tail.

234

He went to shoot a wild duck,
But wild duck flew away;
Says Simon, I can't hit him,
Because he will not stay.

He went to ride a spotted cow,
That had a little calf;
She threw him down upon the ground,
Which made the people laugh.

Once Simon made a great snowball,
And brought it in to roast;
He laid it down before the fire,
And soon the ball was lost.

He went to try if cherries ripe
Did grow upon a thistle;
He pricked his finger very much
Which made poor Simon whistle.

He went for water in a sieve,
But soon it all ran through;
And now poor Simple Simon
Bids you all adieu.

Anonymous

Index of First Lines

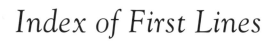